"Robert Leo Heilman's firsthand account of a rural county in Oregon's struggle to keep their libraries open is not unique in a culture and era that is ceasing to value culture—but it is painfully necessary to write of this struggle to document how and what we have become. Hope resides in the many folks who used courage and a democratic process to see this through despite the outcome. Heilman, an accomplished writer, was in the trenches for this one and recounts the struggle concisely."

~James Ross Kelly
Author of *Above Neal Rock*

While Librarians Wept

A Library System Dies 1997–2017

Robert Leo Heilman

A SYLPH MAID BOOK

© 2025 by Robert Leo Heilman

All rights reserved.
No portion of this book may be reproduced in any form
without the prior written permission of the publisher.
Send inquiries to:

Sylph Maid Books
P.O. Box 932
Myrtle Creek, Oregon U.S.A.
97457
(541) 863-5069

ISBN 979-8-89704-113-8

Cover and interior design and composition, copy editing
by Judy Waller
www.johnandjudywaller.com

Cover illustration by Robert Bell

Douglas County Map Source:
https://d-maps.com/carte.php?num_car=83200&lang=en#google_vignette

Printed in the United States of America

The average reader could not possibly understand that every word in that book was a struggle between the writer's mind and a blank piece of paper. If they did, they would genuflect every time they walked into a public library.

~Bill Duncan (1929–2011)
The News-Review
Roseburg, Oregon May 3, 1996

For
Carol Hilderbrand, Patti Rieman and Joy Sanada
My comrades in arms

Contents

Douglas County Data and Map ~ ix–xi

Foreword ~ xiii

Introduction ~ xvii

Archive ~ 1–82
   Columns and Essays:
   pp 1, 10, 16, 32, 40, 45, 52, 55, 58, 61, 63, 69, 82, 87, 100

Epilogue ~ 83

Addendum: Campaign Lessons ~ 95
   Leadership Support ~ 95
   Supporters ~ 96
   Opposition ~ 97
   Tactics ~ 98
   Polling ~ 100

Douglas County Data

DOUGLAS COUNTY, OREGON
2016 U.S. Census Results

Douglas County   pop. 108,244
Cities:
    Canyonville   pop. 2,039
    Elkton   pop. 194
    Drain   pop. 1,167
    Glendale   pop. 877
    Myrtle Creek   pop. 3,409
    Oakland   pop. 929
    Reedsport   pop. 4,051
    Riddle   pop. 1,181
    Roseburg   pop. 22,873
    Sutherlin   pop. 7,954
    Winston   pop. 5,384
    Yoncalla   pop. 1,059

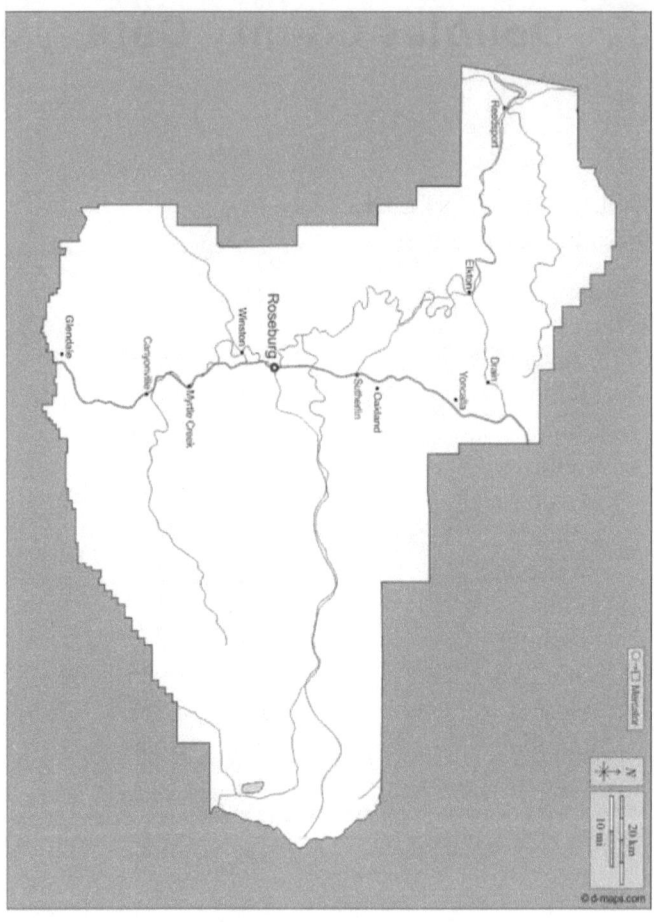

Douglas County Map showing the eleven cities where Douglas County Public Libraries were located.

DOUGLAS COUNTY GOVERNMENT GENERAL FUND EXPENDITURES

Douglas County Library System 1996-2017

Fiscal Year	Nominal	CPIAdjusted2024$USD*
1996–97	$2,026,630.00	$4,060,230.57
1997–98	$1,844,483.00	$3,614,727.00
1998–99	$1,914,088.00	$3,689,076.22
1999–00	$1,936,372.00	$3,653,677.96
2000–01	$1,950,307.00	$3,550,055.35
2001–02	$2,071,807.00	$3,671,358.73
2002–03	$2,211,344.00	$3,862,055.20
2003–04	$2,239,199.00	$3,829,894.80
2004–05	$2,261,268.00	$3,755,328.60
2005–06	$2,539,722.00	$4,088,250.55
2006–07	$2,625,429.00	$4,057,997.24
2007–08	$2,559,429.00	$3,864,842.35
2008–09	$2,217,682.00	$3,659,884.33
2009–10	$1,999,275.00	$2,920,125.56
2010–11	$1,799,211.00	$2,595,849.88
2011–12	$1,430,172.00	$1,991,157.57
2012–13	$1,437,107.00	$1,937,023.76
2013–14	$1,483,658.00	$1,997,764.46
2014–15	$1,499,948.00	$1,980,246.14
2015–16	$1,125,708.00	$1,483,654.97
2016–17	$625,048.00	$817,039.57
2017–18	$0.00	

*Consumer Price Index inflation figures from U.S. Department of Labor Statistics as calculated adjusting for July of each fiscal year start to July 2024.

Foreword

TRYING TO SAVE A LIBRARY

Civilized nations build libraries; lands that have lost their soul close them down.
~Toby Forward

What does a library mean to a community?

"It is a mistake to think of libraries only in terms of their great instrumental value, as a tool, like a screwdriver, to be valued only for their immediate personal utility," wrote Robert Leo Heilman, in response to a question from a newspaper reporter. "Libraries have intrinsic value as well, that is, they have value in their own right as working examples of the goodness of collective generosity and as integral parts of our American cultural identity. They are an important part of who we are, keeping 'urbanity, culture and beauty for its own sake from passing away.'"

This book comprises writings from Heilman's more than twenty years of working to support and save the Douglas County library system—memos and press releases, guest essays and speeches. The book reflects the deep belief in the community value of libraries and the optimism and faith in their neighbors that drove a dedicated group of volunteers to seek solutions, explore compromises, adapt and adjust after years of setbacks.

Early on, library supporters realized that there was little hope to get the conservative county commissioners to continue to squeeze library funding into the ever-shrinking county budget as federal money steadily diminished. They began to study and prepare for presenting county voters with a ballot measure to create an independent library service district to be funded by a tax levy. Eventually they took aim at the May 2012 election.

What followed was a grass roots campaign to build support. They issued press releases, spoke to community groups, wrote opinion pieces for the local daily, encouraged supporters to write letters to the editor and the county commissioners, distributed "I Support My Library" bumper stickers, spoke on local radio shows, met with library boards in several of the cities with branch libraries, held informational meetings at the headquarters library in the county seat, built alliances with key charitable organizations as well as the Democratic Party and the local newspaper, and did speaker tours of key community groups around the county.

Supporters were told the county commissioners would support having the measure on a countywide ballot, only if the city councils in the county's twelve cities would put the independent library district measure on the ballot in their cities. The Save Our Libraries Committee sent representatives to all of those cities. Seven cities passed a resolution to allow their citizens to vote on the measure. Five (with four libraries) did not. Cities that did not have a vote would be excluded from the district. Supporters didn't want to leave those four libraries out of the new district, so, despite polling that showed the measure would have likely prevailed, they decided to scrap the campaign but remained determined to try again in a future election.

County Library System funding declined steadily. Hours were cut and staffing was reduced. There were no county funds for acquiring books and other materials or getting magazine or newspaper subscriptions. Libraries relied on charitable donations to keep up their collection—including from one six-year-old girl who sold cookies for $1 apiece and raised more than $2300.

Heilman and his fellow library supporters continued their public relations campaign to maintain and build support for an independent library district. Part of that was speaking out when alternative "solutions" were proposed, including a merger with the county's history and natural history museum or of "privatizing" the libraries. Those plans, they argued, would weaken the library system's position or undermine the very basis of a free, public library.

In 2015, they started planning to get the independent library district on the November 2016 ballot. They again went to the city councils to get approval to put the measure on the ballot, but they also lobbied the county commissioners and started a petition drive to have the measure put on a countywide ballot, which would preclude the need for the approval of individual cities. They did an economic feasibility study. They won the editorial support of the local newspaper.

The county commissioners agreed to place the measure on the countywide ballot. That was a victory. But it failed 56% to 44%. The effort never did get the support of the county commissioners, and the local Republican Party had supported efforts to defeat it in a year when Donald Trump won 64.6% of the vote in Douglas County.

In July 2017, the countywide library system ceased to be, though remnants of it continue to function with zero county funding and limited hours, reliance on donations, and volunteer staff, many of them participants in the efforts in which Heilman was involved.

Though these library proponents were ultimately unsuccessful, this ground-level view of their efforts provides both models and cautionary tales for other citizens fighting to save their local free public libraries—an all-too-common battle these days—as well as for library science students.

It is an undeniably sad story. But it is also story of citizen heroism against steep odds, an unfavorable political climate, and little support from political leadership. It is a testimony to the ongoing commitment to the fundamental place free public libraries have in their communities that such libraries continue to exist in Douglas County—in admittedly greatly diminished capacities—at all. In offering this history, Heilman clearly hopes that others may learn lessons that can keep more libraries alive.

~Guy Maynard
Author of *The Risk of Being Ridiculous Trilogy*
Eugene, Oregon 2025

Introduction

During one of my daily Save Our Libraries PAC information booth shifts at the 2016 Douglas County Fair, I came to a realization, "Hell, for the amount of time I've put into this effort over the past few years, I could have written another book instead."

This, my fourth book, needs some explanation. Unlike the first three, it is not a consciously literary work but rather, journalism in the form of a personal archive. It is a story of efforts to preserve a countywide library system and of the failure of those efforts. Rather than writing a formal history, I've chosen to tell that story by using my own words as they were written during those years. It is my hope that sharing these guest columns, essays, letters, press releases and memos might prove useful to those who want to secure the future existence of our nation's free public libraries.

From 2011 to 2016 I served on two committees whose aim was to preserve library service for my home, Douglas County, a five thousand square-mile rural place in southwestern Oregon whose borders encompass the Umpqua River system. It is a mountainous place, forested and full of small "shoestring" valleys and some broader bottomland floodplains. Logging and milling timber has been the mainstay of the local economy for generations, especially so ever since the post-World War II GI Bill-fueled housing boom era. From 1950 through 1990 over one billion board feet of timber were cut in the county annually. Comparing this place, which bills itself as "The Timber Capital of the Nation," to Appalachia's coal country is geographically, politically, economically and culturally an apt description.

Over half of the land in the county belongs to the U.S. federal government in the form of U.S. Forest Service National Forest land and in 19th-century railroad and wagon road land-grant acreage controlled by the U.S. Bureau of Land Management. Both agencies make payments to the county government based on the amount of standing timber being sold annually on those lands. It is those payments that allowed the Douglas County government to fund a countywide public library system in 1955. It was also due to those payments that property tax rates in the county became some of the lowest in Oregon, running at about a third of the statewide average.

Two events in the 1990s, and the failure of the county government to respond adequately to them, led to the slow death of the Douglas County Library System on July 1st, 2017 after sixty-one years of service.

The first major factor to come along was the listing of the Northern Spotted Owl as an Endangered Species in June of 1990. Protecting owls and the fish and other critters that depend on old forests for their habitat led to a smaller level of timber cutting and, consequently, smaller payments to Western Oregon counties. This was especially true on the old railway and wagon road land-grant acreage managed by the U.S. BLM. Those lands are known by the collective name "O&C lands," named for the long-defunct Oregon and California Railroad Company which reached Southern Oregon in the 1870s.

O&C payments to counties dropped 30% from 1989 to 1993 when a series of "payments in lieu" of federal timber sales income shares were enacted to help the timber-dependent counties transition to a more sustainable system of funding. This annual system was replaced by the Secure Rural Schools Act and Community Self-Determination Act in 2000. With each renewal of the act the grant money got smaller, forcing county general fund budget cuts while the county commission chose to both lobby and sue the federal government unsuccessfully for increasing federal timber cutting levels. The low old "federal gravy train" property tax rate remained largely in place throughout this long process of diminishing payments.

The second, and most intractable, of these problems was passage of Oregon property tax limitation Measure 5 in November 1990 which was followed by a second one, Measure 50, in 1997. Together, the two changes in taxation created the most serious blow to the county's budget. Measure 5 produced an average 51% reduction in property tax revenue statewide while Measure 50 provided another drop, this time of an additional 11% from the already-reduced levels of 1996. Measure 50 also reduced assessed values of property to 90% of their 1996 amounts and imposed a 3% per annum cap on raising tax assessment values.

The county saw its first Tea Party anti-taxation rally in 2010, held at the county courthouse, and the creation of an Americans for Prosperity chapter that same year. Around that time, robocalls originating in Kansas, the home of the Koch brothers-founded AFP, popped up on local phones with a message opposing passage of a bond measure for the county's community college.

In 2000, fearing an eventual closure of the library system, the Douglas County Library Foundation formed a Library Futures Committee to study the possibility of forming a library service district to fund the county library system through a tax levy. After several years of study, the Futures Committee committed to trying a service district property tax effort in 2011 and put a special district measure up for a vote in 2016. The 2011 proposal never came up for a vote due to several city councils' opposition and a second effort in 2016 failed to pass by 55% to 45% when it appeared on the November general election ballot. That same election found about 70% of the county's voters in favor of electing Donald Trump.

In 1995 Janet Roy, the Myrtle Creek Branch Librarian for the Douglas County Library System, asked me to join the city's Library Advisory Board. What follows are the thousands of words of advocacy that I wrote over the next twenty-one years. Two years later the budget cuts began.

Archive

When the Douglas County Library System was founded in 1955, it consisted of a headquarters library in Roseburg, with eight branch libraries and a bookmobile serving remote parts of the county. The DCLS reported that during the 1956–1957 fiscal year, the first year of operation, the bookmobile completed 94,680 book loans and the eight branch libraries 70,573 more out of a grand total of 305,362 for the system. The county's population that year was roughly 60,000 people.

By the time that the DCLS was shut down in 2017 it consisted of the headquarters library and ten branch libraries, serving a little over 108,000 people. By then, the bookmobile had been gone for twenty years.

VALUE OF COUNTY BOOKMOBILE IS NOT FOUND WITH PENCIL, LEGAL PAD

I grew up surrounded by ledgers, yellow legal pads, #2 pencils, long strips of adding-machine tape and tax forms. My father was a public accountant, my mother is a bookkeeper, my brother is a CPA. Numbers run in the family.

I mention this because it's budget-crunch time here in the Umpqua country and, like my father before me, I fear the seductive power of spreadsheets. "Never let your accountant run your business" was one piece of advice that my dad frequently gave his clients.

Numbers can seem so reliable, standing bedrock

solid in the shifting terrain of tough decisions. Like a solitary butte in a level, hostile desert, they offer us a place to stand and survey the terrain, and a landmark to keep our journey on the right track. Too often though, we mistake them for a destination.

My father knew that the most important elements in the success or failure of a business don't show up in the ledgers. It is the intangibles that make or break you: loyalty to customers and employees, a willingness to forbear enforcing company policies when the situation calls for it, a moral code that consists of something more than just adopting "If it's legal and it's profitable, then it's the right thing to do" as your motto. There are too many other factors, things that might not add up in a penny-shaving climate, but things that will, in the long run, bring you something worth more than the clinking stacks of coins that come with it.

This is true enough in the dog-eat-dog world of business enterprise and even more true in the business of governing where the stakes are incomparably higher. How we spend our tax dollars is not merely an exercise in fiscal responsibility, it determines who we are and sets the limits to what we might become.

In the budget-numbers stampede, where everyone who has an ox out there in the common pasture wants to make sure theirs won't get gored, it's tempting to ignore the intangibles. Those who provide quantifiable services are likely to fare better than those whose good can't be translated into strings of digits.

In the case of an institution like the Douglas County Library system, we can easily show how much it costs us in dollars, roughly $2.2 million per year, but how do you measure the benefits? How many dollars-per-minute is a child's sense of wonder worth? If we could find inspiration, or compassion, or a feeling of self-worth, or understanding, or wisdom sitting on a shelf for sale like a can of beans or a new pair of sneakers, what would be a fair price? We can calculate the cost of providing library services, but that doesn't tell us the value of it.

Our libraries have been asked to make do with $191,000 fewer general fund dollars, a 9% reduction like everyone else. By some measures, that's a huge amount of money being saved, more than many of our county's poorer families can expect to earn in a decade. By other standards, such as the $93 million our county government spent last year, it's chicken feed.

According to the proposed library budget which will be up for consideration soon, we're looking at the following tradeoffs, among others, in order to save ourselves that much in taxes: shutting down the Roseburg Main Branch on Sundays, reducing our ten branch libraries' open hours by an hour or two per week, and eliminating the Bookmobile which serves six of our county's most isolated communities.

Parking the Bookmobile represents $59,200 in costs cut. At nearly a third of the total library budget reduction that pencils out nicely. If it were as simple as that, we could all mutter a collective "Oh, well…" and continue our march towards solvency without so much as a backward glance.

The Bookmobile is more than an expense, more than an investment. It is inextricably woven into who we are. We pride ourselves on being a rural county and resent the power our urban neighbors wield in the legislature.

Now, faced with uncertainty, we're tempted to cut a service to our own most intensely rural communities.

Some folks would say that our library system in general and the Bookmobile in particular are frills we can't afford, given the grim forecast of a declining tax base. If we, the people, are dull, unimaginative and driven by fear, we'll agree. Others, however, will see an opportunity to do something courageous and generous. Some folks would say that the harder we're pressed the more we need to show ourselves and the world that we know the value of things and not just the price.

The News-Review 4/13/1997

I stayed with the Myrtle Creek Citizen Advisory Board through 2003 when the necessity of working away from home in Southern California during five months of the year didn't allow me to effectively serve on that board. I started my third four-year term with the board in 2008 and my fourth term in 2012.

In 2010, out of concern over an ongoing series of county library system budget cuts, I served on the Douglas County Library System Advisory Board. I naively thought that, by serving on both the local and the county-wide levels, I could have more leverage to work against the annual budget cuts. During my time with the DCLS Advisory Board, we were given reports but were never asked for our opinions and were never visited by the system's county commissioner liaison.

While I was with that group, I learned about an effort to pass a property tax base measure that was coming out of the Douglas County Library Foundation's Library Futures Committee. In early 2011, I quit the county advisory board and joined them, handling public and media information for the group.

LETTER TO THE UMPQUA UNITARIAN UNIVERSALIST CONGREGATION 6/14/2011

The Douglas County Library System will be running on greatly reduced hours as of July 1st, 2011. A crippling series of library budget cuts is leaving the system with six fewer employees and, in place of a traditional level of service of forty hours per week, our five largest public libraries (Roseburg, Sutherlin, Reedsport, Winston & Myrtle Creek) will be down to twenty-four hours per week and the six smaller ones (Glendale, Canyonville, Riddle, Oakland, Yoncalla and Drain) will only operate for sixteen hours per week.

At best, next year's county budget will bring a further loss of open-door hours; at worst it may bring a complete shutdown of our entire public library system. Efforts are underway to place a ballot measure before the electorate in the May 2012 local election which would give the Douglas County Library system a secure funding base.

As part of that effort, it is important that we protest these cuts by writing letters to the editors of our local newspapers and to the county board of commissioners during the weeks leading up to July 1st and in the weeks following. So far, to our shame, the landfill Sunday closure has generated more political heat than the loss to our public libraries. It is critically important that our county and city officials hear from us soon.

For further information contact:

Robert Leo Heilman
541-xxx-xxxx.

LETTER TO THE DOUGLAS COUNTY DEMOCRATIC PARTY 6/24/2011

Dear Dems,

As many of you have already heard, the Douglas County Library System is facing crippling budget cuts. The system lost 10% of its funding in 2008, another 10% in 2009, 10% of what was left in 2010 and, for this 2011 fiscal year, a whopping 21% cut.

The past cuts were managed by cutting workers, postponing capital improvements and acquiring fewer books and magazines for the collection. This year's cuts have brought the system to a critical tipping point. Starting July 1st, our five largest branches (Roseburg, Reedsport, Sutherlin, Winston and Myrtle Creek) will be down to 24 hours of service per week and the six smaller ones (Glendale, Canyonville, Riddle, Oakland, Drain and Yoncalla) will be cut back to 16 hours of open-door service per week.

On July 1st, 2012, one of two things will happen to our county's public libraries. If the county receives further O&C Fund Safety Net funding the library system will be merely reduced further, probably on the level of 16 hours per week for the larger libraries and 12 hours for the smaller public libraries. This will be followed by further reductions in the following years. Should the O&C funding dry up altogether, the Douglas County Library System will be shut down completely.

The Library Futures Committee of the Douglas County Library Foundation is planning to place an initiative measure on the May 2012 ballot to establish a library service district with a dedicated tax base that will ensure the system's survival. Passing this measure is the only hope we have of preserving our public libraries. Otherwise, it will be either the immediate shutdown of the entire system or the "death by a thousand cuts."

The political campaign will be firing up in September, with the major portion of the effort coming around Thanksgiving and running right up to the election.

For right now, these next few weeks, the libraries need support in the form of public pressure in the form of letters to the editors of local newspapers. To our shame, the Sunday trash dump closures and the Glide concert have both generated much more political heat than the crippling and potential loss of our public libraries. This leaves the sad impression that no one actually gives a damn about our libraries.

If you want to make the case for restoring funding to our libraries, you should bear in mind that our free public libraries:

Are essential social institutions.

Bring out the best in us.

Are democratically open to one and all.

Are an American invention.

Help to fight illiteracy.

Provide safe shelter to children and the elderly among us.

Are public meeting places.

Are a source of civic pride.

Are helpful to parents who homeschool their kids.

Provide free internet access to people who otherwise would have none at all.

Are increasingly important in the current Great Recession.

Are attractive to companies considering locating

in our county.

And increase real estate values in the cities that have them.

And that:

By reducing or eliminating them we harm the most vulnerable among us—the very old, the very young and the very poor.

The Library Futures Committee meets on the first, second and fourth Tuesdays of the month at 12 noon in the Roseburg Library.

For further information, feel free to contact me.

Peace,

Robert Heilman
541-xxx-xxxx

LET'S PAY UP TO SAVE OUR LIBRARIES

The Douglas County Library system will be facing some unbearably deep cuts in funding soon, cuts which will reduce the entire system to a mere skeleton of itself. It has been proposed that our branch and headquarters libraries keep their doors open for less than half of the hours we now enjoy and that staffing hours be reduced to part-time levels well below what anyone could be expected to pay their bills with. The possibility is very real that we may, shortly after that, close it all down completely, for lack of funding, as has happened in other counties across America.

I love books and I love the libraries that provide them to us. It is a remarkable public service and the great good that our county's libraries make possible is, and has been for generations, an essential building block to our democratic society.

I am not particularly worried about the imminent demise of the Douglas County Library system. I have too much faith in my neighbors here in the One Hundred Valleys to believe that they would allow our libraries to close. To lose our libraries is to confirm the suspicions of our urban critics, who see us as ignorant hayseeds, querulous and out of touch with the finer aspects of culture.

I think we're better than that—better than our neighbors down in Josephine County who lost their library system for a year and only reopened with a sketchy ghost of a system awkwardly run by volunteers.

I think that we're every bit as good as the good folks up in Hood River who recently voted to save their library system by establishing a local tax district to ensure that their libraries will never have to close. A similar proposal is being bandied about now for our home county and I am confident that, once on the ballot, it will pass. Only a handful of mean-spirited misers could possibly refuse to cough up a few bucks every year to keep the pride of the Umpqua intact. We are a generous people here, proud and ornery enough to take responsibility for our own affairs.

The days when we could all kick back and ride the federal timber-payment gravy train for 75% of our county government expenses are over. At some point we all have to grow up and start acting like responsible adults and pay for what we are getting. This should delight conservatives, since it means reducing the size of the federal government's role in our lives and allowing our taxes to be put to use locally, directly for purposes that "we the people" of the Umpqua endorse. Our home here in these mountains needs many things. Surely, we should supply them ourselves, as solid respectable citizens, rather than looking to Washington for a handout, like a bunch of backwoods stew bums.

Whether we like it or not, we're going to have to pay to fix our own potholes, to educate our own children, to dump our own trash in a sanitary landfill and, yes, to safeguard the treasures of our culture and keep them readily available to everyone who lives here.

The News-Review 2/16/2011

PRESS RELEASE:
Event Date: May 25, 2011

Robert Leo Heilman
P.O. Box 932
Myrtle Creek, OR 97457
(541) xxx-xxxx
xxxxxxxxx@mbol.us

MYRTLE CREEK PUBLIC LIBRARY SUPPORT GROUP FORMING

Patrons and supporters of the Myrtle Creek Public Library will meet to organize a local "Friends of the Library" group. The meeting will take place on Wednesday, May 25th, 2011, 7pm at the library, 231 Division St. in Myrtle Creek. Information regarding the upcoming cuts in operating hours at the library from 38 hours per week down to 24 hours per week will be presented as well as plans to help keep the library's doors open in the future. For further information contact:

Robert Heilman
(541) xxx-xxxx

LETTER TO THE FRIENDS OF MYRTLE CREEK LIBRARY #1 6/16/2011

Dear Friends,

I want to thank you all for signing on with the Friends of the Myrtle Creek Public Library. By doing so you are already helping to solve the problem.

I also want to keep you informed about our efforts to get our public library system steady adequate funding. The Library Futures Committee continues to meet three times monthly, on the 1st, 2nd & 4th Tuesdays every month at the Roseburg Library. You are all welcome to drop in and join in the talk. It is a good group.

The Futures Committee has printed 1,000 bumper stickers adorned with the slogan: "I Support My Library." I have picked up ten of these and left them at the Myrtle Creek library so that you can have one of your own. Just stop by and ask Joy or Linda. I will be bringing more of these but for now these ten will have to do for a start. Having them around town for people to see will be a help.

Bob Bell has prepared a newsletter to be sent out by the Futures Committee which will be emailed to you soon. He's done a good job, and I think you'll be pleased.

Diane Williams and I have been invited to talk about the crippling of our library system on a radio show. Daniel Robertson hosts the show, "Progressive Perspectives," which airs on KQEN Monday afternoons from 4pm to 5pm. We are scheduled to spend an hour talking with Daniel on Monday June 27th. Also, I will be recording a radio news commentary about the loss of our library service hours for NPR station KLCC which will air on their news program, "The Northwest Passage" at 4:00–4:30 on Friday, July 1st, the first day of the new budget year and the start of the partial closure of our library.

The next few weeks, leading up to and away from July 1st are a great time to send letters of protest to the Douglas County Board of Commissioners and to *The News-Review*. So far the Sunday closure of the trash dump has generated more political heat than the library closures. A brief, but intense flurry of letters would help us greatly in the year ahead while our silence now will hurt us later, so, please send a brief note out letting them know that you do not approve of this inadequate library budget.

As always, feel free to contact me at any time.

Peace,

Bob Heilman
541-xxx-xxxx
xxxxxxxxx@mbol.us

LETTER TO MYRTLE CREEK LIBRARIAN JOY SANADA 6/29/2011

Dear Joy,

The new website for the library funding campaign is up and running. Bob Bell did a nice job with it. You can visit it at: *keepourlibrariesopen.org*.

Please pass this address on to friends and family. If you have not done so already, please write a short letter to the editor of *The News-Review* or your local weekly newspaper saying that you don't approve of the closing of our libraries.

We are gathering names and addresses and phone numbers for the Library Futures Committee's contact list. If you send me that information for any of your friends, family or acquaintances I will pass that information on to the committee.

Feel free to contact me at any time.

Peace,

Bob Heilman
(541) xxx-xxxx

I suppose that I wrote this next one for Myrtle Creek's little weekly newspaper, but I apparently never submitted it for publication.

DRAFT UNPUBLISHED COLUMN 6/23/2011

Myrtle Creek has something of a reputation for backwardness here in the Umpqua country. It seems that everyone needs someone to look down upon, although I'm not sure why that is. The town certainly has its share of local yahoos, but, having lived in the area for thirty-six years now, I can assure you that it is no more than its fair share. As in any town, whether large or small, its reasonably well-enough educated citizens far outnumber the unreasonable and the ignorant inhabitants.

In at least one way, Myrtle Creek has been a cultural leader for the county. The oldest known library in Douglas County was established here in 1912. It was a local effort, supported by local businesses and private citizens who donated books and money to get it rolling. It was a subscription library, open to the public but requiring an annual membership fee, rather than the free public library system we enjoy today. Details are sketchy but it is believed to have closed down during the Great Depression of the 1930s.

The current Myrtle Creek Public Library was the first public library in Douglas County to offer free internet access to its patrons. Once again, this came about as an entirely local effort. A small handful of people saw the need and made it come about. Frontiernet donated free dial-up internet access, a local citizen donated a computer, others came up with enough money to pay the bill for a dedicated phone line. The whole process took about two or three weeks and was accomplished without writing any grants, and, for that matter, without a single dime coming in from outside the community.

I mention this not just in defense of my neighbors but also in defense of our public library. Both cases of private generosity for the public good show not just the possibilities of philanthropy but also the limitations.

The 1912 library effort, as noble as it was, was limited to serving those who could afford a subscription and to a single town. It lasted as long as it could while depending on the kindness and interest of its citizenry. When hard times came to town it, like much else, folded.

The internet access was limited to a single machine on dial-up. Today, the Myrtle Creek Public Library boasts a set of seven computers and a high-speed wireless internet connection. The improvement has come about due to gifts from the Bill and Melinda Gates Foundation and to the county government providing internet technology services for the entire countywide library system.

We often hear and read about the great good that comes out of our public libraries. They also have a great deal of good coming to them in support from the folks who care so passionately about them, who volunteer their time serving on advisory boards and volunteering with the Douglas County Library Foundation and local Friends of the Library groups.

Well over one hundred volunteers help our libraries by giving of their time and their money to help keep costs down and to ensure a higher level of service than would be possible without them. In itself, this is a great good because it gives people a chance to come together for a purpose that isn't selfish but rather downright generous.

However, all this wonderful voluntary help just isn't enough to sustain a healthy public library system. It takes government funding as well. Here, mired in the midst of the Great Recession, those funds are drying up. Already our libraries are crippled, whittled down to about 60% of their former selves and unless we provide a steady reliable tax base dedicated to their survival, things will certainly get worse.

We reached out to library boards in cities around the county. I was still on the Myrtle Creek board and spoke on behalf of the Futures Committee with the Myrtle Creek, Riddle and Canyonville advisory boards.

MEMO: CITIZENS ADVISORY BOARD INTERVIEWS: CANYONVILLE AND RIDDLE PUBLIC LIBRARIES 6/30/2011

Canyonville

Overall, the Canyonville Board was both positive and enthusiastic. The city council representative was unsure how the city council would vote on putting the measure on their ballot. (Canyonville's council rejected the six cents per thousand OSU Extension measure when it came through). Overall, though, the board feels strongly that the town does care a great deal about their library. What people will do when they vote remains to be seen. The full board and the city council representative were all in attendance.

Q1: Use of library: The group listed borrowing books, use of computers and internet access, children's programs, simple "hanging out," use of the photocopier, book club meetings, reading periodicals and borrowing audio books.

Q2: Consequences of loss of library: Loss of book access, "end of the world," loss of a volunteer opportunity, loss of socializing opportunities, loss of children's exposure to books, loss of their dearly beloved librarian, Carol Hilderbrand.

Q3: Public attitudes: Majority of citizens do care about the library, usage has increased, the idea of the library has great appeal.

Q4: Effective messages: Fear of total loss, break cost down to monthly cost comparison (e.g. one year's taxes equals less than cost of a single hardcover book per month), the chance to increase the collection, the chance to restore open-door hours, patriotism/pride

Q5. Increasing awareness: Flyers, word of mouth/buttonholing, lawn signs, public service announcements.

Riddle

The Riddle board was, overall, more pessimistic than the Canyonville board. They felt that overcoming the strongly held anti-tax ideology common among their neighbors would probably not be possible. The town has high unemployment and poverty rates. The majority of property owners will probably oppose the measure and those who do not own property will be less likely to vote. Only two of the board's members were in attendance and no city council representative was present.

Q1: Use of library: The group listed book club meetings, socializing, the summer reading program for children, computer job searches and other research, education for children/homeschooling, internet access, filing for unemployment benefits and welfare programs such as food stamps, finding "how-to" information, special events such as lectures and the "kill-a-watt" presentation.

Q2: Consequences of loss of library: loss of community identity, loss of access to government programs for poor people, loss of their librarians.

Q3: Public attitudes: Those who use the library love it fiercely, the library is an important source of local pride.

Q4: Effective messages: Economic benefits/self-interest, portray effects of a total loss of services.

Q5: Increasing awareness: Word of mouth, Facebook, consult with politically conservative library users to shape the message.

LETTER TO THE FRIENDS OF MYRTLE CREEK
LIBRARY #2 8/5/2011

Dear Friends,

Douglas County's fiscal year 2011–2012 operating budget s already facing a $3.6 million shortfall—one month after it went into effect. The unexpected reduction comes from a change in the amount of Federal O&C Safety Net funding that will be available to the county from $12 million to $8.4 million.

It is too early to know just how this will affect our public library system but further cuts in service hours are a very real possibility. Early on during last winter's budget negotiations an initial budget proposal based on a 35% reduction to the system's operating costs yielded a proposal calling for operating hours running at sixteen hours per week in the five largest libraries, Reedsport, Sutherlin, Roseburg, Winston and Myrtle Creek and twelve hours per week in Drain, Yoncalla, Oakland, Canyonville, Riddle and Glendale. A later alternative budget calling for a 21% reduction gave us our current hours of twenty-four open-door service hours in the larger branches and sixteen at the smaller libraries. While it is not certain that the shorter service hours schedule will be adopted, it is likely that something along those lines will have to be put in place in order to balance the county's budget. I will let you know how this turns out as soon as we know the results.

The Douglas County Library Foundation's Library Futures Committee has scheduled a smallish informational meeting for September 1st from 3pm–5pm at the Roseburg Library's Ford Meeting Room. The hope is to draw a small group of thirty or so influential citizens from throughout the county so that we can educate them about the problems facing our county public library system and to ask for their suggestions on what they feel ought to be done to help save our libraries. If you know someone who you think should attend, please send me their name and contact information and I will pass that along to the committee.

I do hope that you all have visited the *www.keepourlibrariesopen.org* website and have entered your email address in the "subscription" box. This will put you on the Futures Committee mailing list and allow you to receive their Newsletter.

Bumper stickers reading, "I Support My Library" are available for free at our library. They are printed on plastic and have a low-tack adhesive which will not mess up your paint when you remove them.

For those of you with high-speed access to the web, the following "Biblioburro" YouTube video from Columbia says a great deal about the usefulness of libraries:

www.youtube.com/watch?v=wuTswmx9TQU

Also, I have changed web services and have a new email address: xxxxxxxxx@frontier.com

Well, that's about all the news that fits, for now. I will be sending another note to you all (we now have 20 members) once we understand the effects of this new budgetary crisis. As always, feel free to contact me at any time.

Peace,

Bob Heilman
(541) xxx-xxxx

MEMO: TO THE LIBRARY FUTURES COMMITTEE
RE: MEETING WITH RIDDLE MAYOR BILL DUCKETT

Mr. Duckett seems to be a strong supporter of libraries which he classifies as "essential to any community." He is positive that the Riddle City Council will approve a resolution to allow a library service district measure on the Riddle city ballot. He feels that a library service district measure would probably pass in Riddle, though narrowly. He recommends "Lots of positive information," as the best way to persuade the voters, "Let them know about the benefits ahead of time and they will come around."

He spoke warmly and knowledgeably about the good work of libraries, mentioning socializing, research, internet access, wi-fi access, and the role of libraries in preserving our history and culture.

The meeting took place at Riddle City Hall on 12 September 2011. He was interviewed by Robert Heilman.

Archive

LETTER TO CANYONVILLE LIBRARY ADVISORY BOARD 9/12/2011

As you know, we are getting close to a critically important decision on whether or not The Canyonville Public Library will still be open a year from now. On November 21st we will be asking the Canyonville City Council to approve a resolution allowing the citizens of Canyonville to vote in the May 2012 election on whether or not to establish a library service district.

A "yes" majority vote allows the measure to be placed on the city ballot; a "no" majority vote closes the library. That is, if the resolution passes we have a chance to keep the library but failing to pass it means that even if the rest of the Douglas County Library System's branches remain open, Canyonville's will not. The most likely result of the "no" vote is that patrons of the Canyonville Public Library who live outside the city limits will be able to use the other library branches free of charge, but residents of Canyonville will have to pay a yearly subscription fee for their "Out of District" access.

So, what follows are suggestions about how to help keep your library open:

Friends of the Library:

Reviving the Canyonville Friends of the Library group would be helpful. Pick a date for an organizational meeting, get the word out about it through the newspaper and flyers and a sign-up list at the library. If your library has a book club ask them to join as a group. Enroll as many people as you can. Be sure to get their names, phone numbers and email addresses. Ask them to "talk it up" around town, letting their neighbors know that the library is in danger of being closed. Ask them to show up at the city council meeting. They will be helpful, later on as well, when the ballot measure campaign takes off.

Petition:

You might want to ask your Friends group to help gather signatures for a non-binding local petition urging the city council to support the library and present that to the council at the meeting. This will put you in contact with people you don't already know, help raise awareness and give the council something to think about when they consider the resolution. Strong public support goes a long way in overcoming political opposition.

At the meeting:

Filling the room with supporters is very useful. Bring as many children as you can. Force them to look at the parents, grandparents and children who will be affected by a library closure. Testify, briefly but assertively. Talk up the benefits and the consequences of closure but keep returning to the theme: "Let us vote." "Let the public decide this one." "Please don't take away our right to vote."

LETTER FOR THE FRIENDS OF MYRTLE CREEK LIBRARY #3 9/20/2011

Dear Friends,

Well, summer has been here and gone, and we are entering a busy season this fall for our efforts to preserve the Douglas County Library System.

The Library Futures Committee of the Douglas County Library Foundation held a small meeting on September 1st. About 30 local people, whom the committee considered "prominent" in the county, attended and were presented with information about the sorry state of our endangered library system. We drew strong support from the crowd, both as individuals and as organizations and businesses. Some of our "allies" include the Ford Family Foundation, The Whipple Trust, Creative Images, *The News-Review* and the Democratic Party of Douglas County.

Probably the most significant news is that a Political Action Committee (PAC) is being formed, even as I write this, for the purpose of promoting a ballot measure which will create a countywide library service district with steady funding through its own tax base.

In its current form, the system has never been funded by the county's General Fund, but supported instead by Federal timber-sales payments (1955–1995), and since 1996, by the so-called "Safety Net" payments in lieu of timber-sales payments. With those payments very likely to stop completely at the end of this fiscal year (30 June, 2012), the county will not have enough income to keep our libraries open. Therefore, we will be placing a measure on the May 2012 election ballot to keep the doors open.

I cannot give you a solid figure yet as to the property-tax rate that we will be asking our neighbors to approve but it will be somewhere between 35 cents per thousand and 50 cents per thousand dollars of assessed property value. We will have an exact figure soon, during the first week of October, after the completion of a study which is being conducted by the Library Futures Committee. At the moment, though, it appears that it will probably be something close to 40 cents per thousand.

During the months of October and November we will be visiting all twelve of our county's city councils and asking them to allow the service district measure to be placed on their city ballots. This is a critically important step in trying to preserve our eleven-library system. If any of the cities fail to approve putting the measure up for a vote on their ballots those cities will lose their libraries— whether or not the measure passes countywide. So, a "Yes" vote allows each local branch library a chance for survival but a "No" vote will certainly close that branch library as of July 1st, 2012. Residents of those cities which fail to carry the ballot will then be considered "out-of-district" users and charged something on the order of $50 per year to use those libraries which are still open.

Our locally scheduled city council meetings are: Myrtle Creek on October 18th 7pm; Riddle November 14th at 7:30pm; Canyonville November 21st at 7pm. The measures are expected to pass in Myrtle Creek and Riddle, but Canyonville's vote is uncertain. Please try to attend some or all of these meetings. If you do attend be sure to note your support for the library next to your signature when you sign in. The more that we can "talk this up" among our family, friends and neighbors, the more likely it will be that we can get this measure on the ballots and passed by the voters.

The Library Futures committee has hired a woman

by the name of Ginger Nickel who will be going around the county from now until the end of December on a speaking tour on behalf of our library system. She is looking for groups to speak to such as local Chambers of Commerce, school faculty meetings, church groups and social organizations like the Lions and Rotary clubs. If you want her to come and talk to your group, please contact her via email: xxxxxxxxxxxx@yahoo.com.

We have inherited about a thousand campaign lawn signs from the Hood River Library System. They are red signs with yellow lettering and trim which read "Library Yes!' with the traditional ballot checkmark. I have them stored here at my place and they will be handy when the political campaign kicks in after the December holidays.

If you haven't done so, please stop by the library and pick up an "I Support My Library" bumper sticker. The stickers are made with a low-tack adhesive that makes removal easy and will not harm your paint. Also, do visit our website: keepourlibrariesopen.org and enter your email address in the little "subscribe" box. This will allow the campaign to send you updates and a monthly newsletter.

I want to be sure to thank each of you for taking an interest in this effort. Just by signing up with the Friends of the Myrtle Creek Public Library and keeping yourself informed you have already helped.

As always, feel free to contact me with any concerns, suggestions or questions about this effort.

Peace,

Bob Heilman
(541) xxx-xxxx
xxxxxxxxx@frontier.com

That Fall of 2011, the committee made appeals to the eleven city governments that had DCLS libraries, asking for the ballot measure to appear on their city ballots. Without city council approval, the town's citizens would not be able to vote either for or against the measure. I took on the job of talking to three small neighboring cities, Myrtle Creek (pop. 3,439), Riddle (pop. 1,185) and Canyonville (pop. 1,640).

COVER LETTER TO MYRTLE CREEK CITY MANAGER 10/10/2011

Library Futures Committee
Members: Jim Williams (Chair), Bob Bell, Robert Leo Heilman, Charlotte Herbert, Max Leek, Jim Pratt, Jeff Pugh, Penny Reed, Lois Soulia, Penny Tannlund, Karen Tolley, Diane Williams, Kathy Vejtasa

October 10, 2011

Aaron Cubic, City Administrator
City of Myrtle Creek
207 NW Pleasant Street
P.O. Box 940
Myrtle Creek, OR 97457

Dear Mr. Cubic,

Enclosed are eight packets of material in support of a presentation I will make to the Myrtle Creek City Council on October 18. I will speak in support of a resolution to place a library funding measure on the ballot for the May 15, 2012, election. The formal text reads "Resolution Approving Douglas County Order to Initiate Formation of County Library System Service District."

The Futures Committee met last Tuesday, October

4th and reviewed three different library plans/budgets (which differ mainly in the number of hours the county libraries will be open and the size of the materials budget). We determined that an effective but lean library can be funded for a maximum cost of $.50/$1,000. An overview of what the system will look like is in the packets for the Council.

If you need further information, please feel free to contact me.

Sincerely,

Robert Leo Heilman
xxxx Weaver Rd.
Myrtle Creek, OR 97457
(541) xxx-xxxx
xxxxxxxxx@frontier.com

The 2011 effort collapsed when five of the eleven cities that we approached refused to allow the measure to be put up for a vote. Of the three cities that were my assignment, Riddle's council did approve placing it on their city ballot, but Myrtle Creek and Canyonville did not. In Myrtle Creek, the council tabled the motion at a second meeting ending all further discussion; in Canyonville the proposal died for lack of a second to the initial motion.

At that time, all twelve of the county's cities had recently been notified by the federal government that their water and sewage treatment plants needed multimillion-dollar upgrades in order to meet Environmental Protection Agency standards and were reluctantly looking at large and unavoidable sanitary district usage rate hikes for their citizens.

SAVE OUR LIBRARIES COMMITTEE WENT TO COUNCILS OUT OF RESPECT

The effort to create a library service district with stable funding for our county has been abandoned—at least for now. Our proposed ballot measure will not come before the voters in the May 2011 general election. It was a difficult decision for our committee to make but we are convinced that it was the right thing to do.

In order to put the measure on the ballot we needed the approval of our county's city councils. The proposed service district must have boundaries, and no incorporated area can be included within the district unless its residents vote to approve their inclusion. The residents, however, cannot vote at all unless their city councils approve placing the matter before them on their city's ballot.

We approached all of the twelve cities in Douglas County and asked them to pass a resolution allowing their citizens to vote. Seven of them passed the resolution while five did not. Without the participation of those five cities, we simply could not go forward with the measure. The Douglas County Board of Commissioners was not at all likely to place the matter on the countywide ballot and, frankly, we were very reluctant to leave four of our eleven libraries excluded from the proposed district.

The service district, had it been placed on the May election ballot and then passed, would have served 83% of the county's population and could have drawn on 88% of the proposed full tax base. It is likely that some, at least, of the uncooperative cities would have joined the district after it was created, but how many of them that would have been we cannot know.

Neither did we know just what would happen to those four libraries, three of which were among our five largest and busiest branches. It is possible that they would have all been closed, or that some would have been closed. In any case, the 17% of the population that was outside the new district would have been ineligible to receive free public library services.

It was, and remains, our goal to preserve the integrity of our entire library system of eleven libraries. We feel that we all, as residents of this county, should take part in deciding whether we are willing to pay for the great good that the Douglas County Library System provides. Unfortunately, a handful of city councils did not agree with us and chose instead to prevent their citizens from voting on the matter.

The decision was made even more painful

for us by the results of an opinion poll which we commissioned, and which was conducted near the end of our city council resolution campaign. We knew that, had the measure been voted on during the second week in December 2011 our library service district measure would have passed with strong support. The numbers were consistent across the county, urban and rural voters, voters in the north end of the county, the central part and in the south, all would have passed the measure by the same margin. The poll results predicted a victory margin of 57% in favor of funding our public libraries through a property tax increase to 43% opposed.

It is heartening that we, the people of the Umpqua, have shown ourselves to be generous citizens who are willing to pay for this essential community service. It is our intention to bring this library service district measure forward again in the hope that we can persuade all of our city councils to trust in the wisdom of their citizens.

The News-Review 12/6/2011

LIBRARY SURVEY EXTRACTIONS

Method:

The Douglas County Library Foundation's Library Futures Committee commissioned a telephone survey of Douglas County voters to determine their attitudes toward the county's library system and their willingness to support the system through a property tax levy of fifty cents per thousand dollars of assessed value.

The survey was conducted during the weeks covering December 4th through December 17th, 2011. Roughly 4,000 voters were contacted and among them, 586 were kind enough to give their opinions in response to the questions. The survey's results are reasonably proportional geographically. For example, the City of Myrtle Creek makes up 3.2% of the county's population and answers from Myrtle Creek voters make up 2.55% of the survey responses.

All of those contacted were registered voters who had voted in at least three of the last four general elections. Homeowners made up 75% of those who took part in the survey and the majority of the voters surveyed had been living in Douglas County, Oregon for twenty years or more. 86% of the respondents were older than forty years of age.

KEY:

Urban: All twelve Douglas County cities
Rural: All unincorporated areas of Douglas County except for: Line #08, "Unincorporated Roseburg" which is included with Roseburg City data.
Countywide: All of Douglas County
Small Towns: Elkton, Drain, Yoncalla, Oakland, Riddle,

Canyonville & Glendale, which host our six smaller branch libraries.

North County: Elkton, Drain, Yoncalla, Oakland & Sutherlin (Reedsport not included)

South County: Winston, Myrtle Creek, Riddle, Canyonville & Glendale

Election Result: Predicted election final result, based on the relative percentages of "Yes" and "No" responses for Q5.

*R5: Elkton, Sutherlin, Winston, Myrtle Creek & Canyonville whose city councils did not pass the service district resolution.

Q1: Importance of the County Library System

	Very		Somewhat		Neutral		Not Very		Not	
Canyonville*	7	(88%)	0		1	(12%)	0		0	
Drain	9	(90%)	1	(10%)	0		0		0	
Elkton*	0		0		1	(100%)	0		0	
Glendale	3	(100%)	0		0		0		0	
Myrtle Creek*	9	(60%)	4	(27%)	2	(13%)	0		0	
Oakland	3	(60%)	1	(20%)	1	(20%)	0		0	
Reedsport	18	(67%)	5	(19%)	1	(14%)	0		2	(8%)
Riddle	3	(60%)	2	(40%)	0		0		0	
Roseburg	129	(81%)	26	(16%)	2	(1%)	1	(0.5%)	2	(1%)
Sutherlin*	31	(74%)	7	(17%)	2	(5%)	1	(2%)	1	(2%)
Winston*	20	(70%)	5	(17%)	1	(3%)	2	(7%)	1	(3%)
Yoncalla	5	(100%)	0		0		0		0	
Urban	267	(79%)	51	(15%)	11	(3%)	4	(1%)	6	(2%)
Rural	178	(72%)	52	(21%)	11	(4%)	5	(2%)	2	(1%)
Countywide	445	(76%)	103	(18%)	22	(4%)	9	(2%)	8	(1%)
Small Towns	28	(80%)	4	(11%)	3	(9%)	0		0	
North County	45	(78%)	8	(14%)	3	(5%)	1	(2%)	1	(2%)
South County	42	(70%)	11	(18%)	4	(6%)	2	(3%)	1	(2%)
*R5	67	(71%)	16	(17%)	7	(7%)	3	(3%)	2	(2%)

Q4: Awareness of the Proposed Measure

	Yes	No	No Reply
Canyonville*	4 (50%)	4 (50%)	0
Drain	3 (30%)	7 (70%)	0

	Yes	No	No Reply
Elkton*	0	1 (100%)	0
Glendale	2 (66%)	1 (34%)	0
Myrtle Creek*	8 (53%)	6 (40%)	1 (7%)
Oakland	3 (60%)	2 (40%)	0
Reedsport	10 (38%	16 (62%)	0
Riddle	3 (60%)	2 (40%)	0
Roseburg	84 (53%)	74 (46%)	2 (1%)
Sutherlin*	18 (43%)	24 (57%)	0
Winston*	15 (52%)	12 (41%)	2 (7%)
Yoncalla	2 (40%)	3 (60%)	0

	Yes	No	No Reply
Urban	152 (49%)	152 (49%)	5 (2%)
Rural	142 (51%)	129 (46%)	7 (3%)
Countywide	294 (51%)	129 (46%)	7 (3%)
Small Towns	17 (46%)	22 (54%)	0
North County	26 (41%)	37 59%)	0
South County	32 (53%)	25 (42%)	3 (5%)
*R5	45 (54%)	36 (43%)	3 (2%)

Q5: Willingness to Vote Yes on the Measure

	Yes	No	Undecided
Canyonville*	4 (50%)	3 (38%)	1 (2%)
Drain	3 (30%)	3 (30%)	4 (40%)
Elkton*	0	1 (100%)	0
Glendale	3 (100%)	0	0
Myrtle Creek*	7 (47%)	4 (27%)	4 (27%)
Oakland	3 (60%)	2 (40%)	0
Reedsport	11 (44%	11 (44%)	4 (12%)
Riddle	3 (60%)	2 (40%)	0
Roseburg	91 (56%)	54 (33%)	18 (11%)
Sutherlin*	17 (40%)	22 (52%)	3 (7%)
Winston*	13 (45%)	9 (31%)	7 (24%)
Yoncalla	1 (20%)	2 (40%)	2 (40%)
Urban	156 (50%)	113 (36%)	43 (14%)
Rural	127 (46%)	99 (36%)	49 (18%)
Countywide	283 (48%)	212 (36%)	92 (16%)
Small Towns	17 (46%)	13 (35%)	7 (19%)
North County	24 (38%)	30 (48%)	9 (14%)
South County	30 (50%)	25 (42%)	3 (5%)
*R5	45 (54%)	18 (30%)	12 (20%)

In the spring of 2012, I wrote a note for the Library Futures Committee to distribute to library supporters.

LIBRARY SYSTEM GIVEN REPRIEVE BUT YOUR SUPPORT IS STILL NEEDED

Our Douglas County commissioners have committed to funding our library system at the current level for another year. This is good news in that there will be no further reductions in open-door hours and none of our branch libraries will be closed—at least not yet.

Budget cuts over the past five years have reduced the system to about 60% of the service it used to provide. In early budget meetings with the commissioners, DCLS Director Max Leek was able to convince them that further reducing the library system's budget could not be done without closing at least some of our 10 branch libraries. The commissioners have asked Mr. Leek to prepare a budget for the fiscal year 2012–2013 which keeps all branches open and maintains current hours of operation.

While we are pleased to hear that we will not be facing the shutting-down of the system in the next county budget cycle, the reprieve means that our libraries will be still stuck with an inadequate budget for another twelve months. As it is, the system has virtually no budget for purchasing books for the collection or newspaper and magazine subscriptions. The collection has been deteriorating for the past few years and although private donations have risen, they still are not nearly adequate to keep the collection growing.

There are no guarantees of steady funding beyond

the next fiscal year. Federal funding of the county government is still in doubt and the system is likely to continue to lose skilled employees as they seek full-time reliable income elsewhere.

We remain committed to establishing steady adequate funding for our libraries and the commissioners' decision is only temporary and does not meet the demand for library services.

The county budget process is underway, with hearings scheduled through the month of May and the final decisions to be announced in June. Now is a good time to contact the Douglas County Board of Commissioners to urge them to restore the library system's hours.

God bless old Bill Duncan (1929–2011), a thoroughly honorable man: U.S. Marine Corps veteran and a man whose decades-long newspaper career included the jobs of reporter, photojournalist, columnist, editor, publisher, author and community college writing instructor.

OF OUR TRASH AND OUR CULTURE

The late Bill Duncan wrote a column last year during the annual county budget hearings expressing his disappointment that there seemed to be a great deal more political heat over cutting hours at the county landfill than for losing hours in our county's library system. It was a good column, one that made an important point about our puzzling priorities when it comes to paying for public services.

Looking back on it, I am haunted by thoughts about how the political heat at the time affected the outcome of those budget decisions to close the landfill an extra day per week and to cripple the library system.

The failure to put a fee system in place for our trash disposal has left us with less service and an unnecessary $1.4 million drain on the county's general fund. Charging dump fees has long been the poison oak of Douglas County politics, something no one has wanted to touch. Yet, from a fiscal (and moral) standpoint, it is obviously the right thing to do. With a bit of persuasive leadership, I believe that the majority of us here in the One Hundred Valleys would be in favor of paying to clean up our own messes.

As Mr. Duncan pointed out, there was a good deal of grousing going on, as there always is whenever any government seems like it is ready to dip into its citizens' pockets. It was a case of "the squeaky wheel" once again "getting the grease." A relative handful of chronic malcontents, the tightwads and "no-tax" ideologues among us, whined loudly about it and so our county government caved in to their peevishness.

At the same time, our libraries faced a severe cut in funding, one that left us with what amounts to 60% of a library system. Very few people, less than a handful it seems, spoke up at the time on behalf of what is probably the best-loved service that our county government provides. The political wisdom of the moment concluded that since no one seemed to care, the libraries could safely be forced to starve into near collapse.

As it turned out, the citizens of Douglas County Oregon do care about their libraries. Last December's polling for the proposed creation of a countywide library service district funded by a property tax base of fifty cents per thousand dollars of assessed value showed strong support for the idea. The poll predicted that such a measure would almost certainly pass.

Unfortunately, the Library Futures Committee, the measure's sponsor, was unable to persuade city councils in Elkton, Sutherlin, Winston, Myrtle Creek and Canyonville to allow their citizens to vote on the matter. In each of those cities there was a feeling among city councilors that the majority of their voters would be opposed to paying for the services they receive from the library. In actuality, the majority of voters in at least four of those towns (as in the rest of the county) were actually in favor of the proposal.

One of the more common complaints among the

city councils in all twelve Douglas County cities was that the county commissioners were refusing to support the measure. In fact, at least two of our commissioners were pessimistic about the chances of such a measure passing and felt that the effort to bring it to the voters was, at best, an unnecessary waste of time.

Had the Douglas County Board of Commissioners been openly supportive of the library service district proposal—as county commissioners in several other Oregon counties have been in the past—it is likely that the measure would have been on the May ballot this year and that it would have passed, saving the county general fund another $1.5 million.

We are facing the loss of last year's federal "safety net" funding. Instituting the dump fees and passing the library service district measure would have cut that shortfall by about $3 million. We would also have had full service from both the county landfill system and at all eleven of our county libraries.

In these two decisions we have seen a case of misguided political expediency. Politics, of course, is something of an art. It is no wonder that mistakes are often made when deciding matters on the basis of what does or does not seem to be a popular opinion at the moment.

There is, however, the art of leadership to consider as well. It is an art which requires enough insight to know what is right and what is wrong and the courage to do what is right, even if it seems unpopular.

The News-Review 3/2/2012

Little Lolly's efforts gained national attention. Umpqua Community College writing instructor and artist Diane Williams made a framed pen-and-ink-with-watercolor certificate of appreciation for her, and lawyer Jeff Pugh did the presentation.

RELEASE

Event Date: 24 March 2012
Location: Main Stage, Spring Fair, Douglas County
    Fairgrounds, Douglas Building, Roseburg OR
Time: Sometime between 11:30am and 12:30pm

SIX-YEAR-OLD TO RECEIVE OUTSTANDING VOLUNTEER AWARD FROM LIBRARY FOUNDATION

Lolly Frost, a six-year-old girl from Drain, Oregon will receive an award from the Douglas County Library Foundation for her fundraising efforts on behalf of the Drain Public Library. Lolly has been baking cookies and selling them for $1.00 each to raise funds for her local library. Lolly uses a small child's cookie-baking appliance with a capacity of nine cookies per batch.

Since the start of this year, Lolly's cookies have raised over $2,300 to help purchase books and magazine subscriptions for the Drain Public Library's collection.

Due to budget cuts, the Douglas County Library System now depends almost exclusively on private donations in order to replace damaged books, purchase new books and renew magazine subscriptions.

Lolly, who is a homeschooled first-grade student, is a frequent user of the library. Upon hearing of the library's budget troubles, she decided to help out by raising money. Lolly's effort caught the attention of

PremierWest Bank branch in Drain. The bank now sells Lolly's cookies to their customers. For the first 250 of her cookies sold there the bank adds an extra $4.00 to the fund, raising the benefit from those cookie sales to $5 each.

The award will be presented by Jeff Pugh, President of the Douglas County Library Foundation.

INFO:
Lolly's mother, Xxx Xxxxx, can be contacted at:
xxxxxxxxxxxxxx@yahoo.com

The News-Review has printed two articles on Lolly's baking:
www.nrtoday.com

Robert Leo Heilman
541-xxx-xxxx
xxxxxxxxx@frontier.com

In Spring, 2012, the Oregon Library Association asked me to write an essay for their OLA Quarterly *magazine. I plagiarized the ending but decided that plagiarizing my own work is, at worst, a very minor sin for a writer.*

AT YOUR SERVICE

I was delighted to hear that Carol Hilderbrand had been named "Educator of the Year" at the annual Citizen of the Year banquet. I've known her for nearly thirty years now in our small-town way, and the good news first struck me as both a well-deserved honor and an unexpected one.

Carol is a librarian who presides over the Canyonville Public Library and though she is not a teacher or professor, I saw immediately the justice of the award. She spends her working days helping people, in a dozen ways, to get the knowledge that drew them to her small section of city hall. It is heartening to watch her patient and skillful work in greeting the patrons, taking the time to listen to their worries and hopes, their joys and sorrows, and always her gentle suggestions for sources of further information or amusement.

It was only later that I remembered the cuts. At the moment when Carol was being honored, her library was facing a severe budget cut. A few months later, the Canyonville Public Library lost six of its weekly twenty-two open-door hours—a major loss not just in library service but to the well-being of the town. A few months after that, her small town's city council refused to allow a measure aimed at giving the library system a steady and adequate tax base to be placed on their ballot, a decision which left Carol's library with a serious risk of permanent closure.

Getting people to understand the great social value of our free public libraries has become increasingly difficult over the past twenty years. I have heard it argued that maintaining a library at public expense is a waste of tax revenue in this age of easy internet access. This line of reasoning always seems to come from people who are perfectly able to pay the small necessary annual tax and who haven't actually set foot in a public library for several years. If a public library was a mere tool, like a screwdriver, a dictionary or the internet, such talk would be reasonable. Fortunately, our free public libraries are much more than that.

Both the internet and the library are sources of information. The difference is that the virtual help offered by the world-wide web is impersonal, while libraries have librarians. When you walk in the door of your local public library there is someone there who is ready to help you. Librarians aren't there to run a scam on you, nor to try to turn a profit, or to deceive you— all of which are common-enough occurrences in this, the so-called "information age." A librarian is more than just a specialist but rather a sort of friend to one and all, someone with nothing more than your own good at heart.

We live in an age of epidemic loneliness. Along with our gadgets and our wealth have come increasing isolation and alienation. Our virtual magic carpets have whisked us off to illusory worlds with much to delight the eye and the intellect but little to please our hearts. I have often, over the years, thought of our free public libraries as temples of knowledge. It is only lately that I have come to understand that they are temples of compassion as well.

The creation of free public libraries is, in itself, a compassionate act. Properly understood, compassion is a matter of acknowledging that others are equal to us and therefore deserving of the same respect and kindly assistance that we would accord ourselves. Compassion is an essentially egalitarian approach to living and our free public libraries first came about as a way to extend that personal compassion to entire communities. A public library is one of the few places that I know of where I am always treated with real respect, as an equal rather than as a mere consumer or client, patient or employee.

I am, I admit, quite fond of librarians. Of course, as a writer of literature, public libraries and their librarians are useful to my career and, as such, would deserve my support and respect if only as a matter of self-interest. But my trust and admiration for these institutions and their staffs goes beyond mere pecuniary concerns. B. Traven, one of the Twentieth Century's great literary lights, once described the world's artists as "… the small army which is the salt of the earth, and which keeps culture, urbanity and beauty for its own sake from passing away." Librarians are more than just my allies in our society's struggle against ignorance and barbarism, they are artists in their own right and my comrades in arms.

They, alone among the professional classes, have consistently earned my admiration throughout my life. Nearly everything that I know I learned because I read it in a book, and nearly all of those thousands of books came from either a public library or from the racks of used books in the back of second-hand stores. I have lived long enough at the bottom of the societal heap to have seen oppression in both its gross and petty forms and to have learned from it a deep-seated distrust of the credentialed products of what passes for "higher education" in our society. It has often struck me that "the evil that men do" in these modern days, is mostly done by those who hold advanced college degrees. Yet, when I contemplate the horrible mediocrity of our mass culture and the terrible pain brought to so many through their inescapable poverty and through the cold-blooded ill treatment that is their daily share, it comes to me that librarians, at least, are consistently creative and helpful people.

We seldom know the full worth of the good we do. A kind word or an offhand suggestion at the right time can often save a life or launch a useful career. The people we meet in our daily lives remain largely mysterious to us. A stranger met once may never be met again and yet the memory of that meeting may affect their lives or ours for decades afterward, perhaps enriching a life or two or thousands of other lives. The front desk of a public library is not just a place where such things can happen. It is a place whose purpose is to make sure that it will happen—repeatedly and "for the common good."

The premise underlying free public libraries is neither a liberal nor a conservative reason for having them. It is, however, an American premise: That all of us need to have an equal opportunity to educate ourselves. I like to think of them as both the university of the poor and the place where the truly educated go to continue to learn. It is obvious that an education through a process which aims at obtaining accreditation is a very inferior sort of education, one that at best prepares us to learn on our own. And where but in a public library can a thorough lifelong education take place free of charge and assisted by a kindly neighbor?

"Greed is good," I've heard it said by people who seem to believe that naked self-interest is what drives all human relations. I often wonder what they think of the other six deadly sins. Do they believe that anger, lust, gluttony, sloth, pride and envy are also good? It is important to note that "sloth" in the classical theological sense refers not to physical laziness but to a state of profound indifference. It is distressing to me that we live in a radically libertarian age of rampant tightwadism and sad that our free public libraries should be closed because of "bottom line" small-mindedness.

I grew up surrounded by ledgers, yellow legal pads, #2 pencils, long strips of adding-machine tape and tax forms. My father was a public accountant, my mother is a bookkeeper, my brother is a CPA as is one of my nieces. Numbers run in the family. I mention this because, like my father before me, I fear the seductive power of spreadsheets. "Never let your accountant run your business" was one piece of advice that my dad frequently gave his clients.

Numbers can seem so reliable, standing bedrock solid in the shifting terrain of tough decisions. Like a solitary butte in a level, hostile desert they offer us a place to stand and survey the terrain, and a landmark to keep our journey on the right track. Too often though, we mistake them for a destination.

My father knew that the most important elements in the success or failure of a business don't show up in the ledgers. It is the intangibles that make or break you: loyalty to customers and employees, a willingness to forbear enforcing company policies when the situation calls for it, a moral code that consists of something more than adopting "If it's legal and it's profitable, then it's the right thing to do" as your motto. There are too many other factors, things that might not add up in a penny-shaving climate, but things that will, in the long run, bring you something worth more than a transitory increase in profits.

This is true enough in the dog-eat-dog world of business enterprise and even more true in the business of governing, where the stakes are incomparably higher. How we spend our tax dollars is not merely an exercise in fiscal responsibility, it determines who we are and sets the limits to what we might become.

In the budget-numbers stampede, where everyone who has an ox out there in the common pasture wants to make sure theirs won't get gored, it's tempting to ignore the intangibles. Those who provide quantifiable services are likely to fare better than those whose good cannot (and perhaps shouldn't) be translated into strings of digits.

In the case of an institution like a library system, we can easily show how much it costs us in dollars, but how do you measure the benefits? How many dollars-per-minute is a child's sense of wonder worth? If we could find inspiration, or compassion, or a feeling of self-worth, or understanding, or wisdom sitting on a shelf for sale like a can of beans or a new pair of sneakers, what would be a fair price? We can calculate the price of providing library services, but that doesn't tell us the value of it.

Must all the public good that can't be expressed by strings of digits and displayed on a spreadsheet lose public funding? Have we, as a society, concluded at last that we must abandon generosity and compassion in order to prosper? Not so very long ago, these were said to be the essential ingredients in the humane glue that holds us together as a nation and as a people.

OLA Quarterly, Fall
Oregon Library Association 9/1/2012

In the Fall of 2012, one of the county commissioners, Susan Morgan, proposed combining the Douglas County Library System and the Douglas County Museum of History and Natural History into a single agency under the direction of the museum director to save the county some budget money. Susan was the board's liaison for the museum and Doug Robertson was the liaison for the DCLS.

UNPUBLISHED COLUMN *circa October 2012 and laid to rest unsent and unfinished as-is after this unworkable proposal quickly failed due to pressure from library supporters and the State Librarian of Oregon who pointed out that the proposed merger would have a director who lacked a Master of Library Science degree.*

At first glance, the proposal to merge the Douglas County Library system with the Douglas County Museum of History and Natural History seems like it might be a workable proposal. The two county departments do have similar goals of making information available to the public and of preserving our culture for future generations. Yet, when you look into the consequences of such a merger, the potential problems grow quickly in both numbers and size, while the likely benefits shrink, if not in numbers, then at least in the amount of good they might bring.

Both county departments are struggling to provide service, having been crippled by serious budget cuts. The library system is already dying a slow death due to inadequate funding. The current budget does not allow our libraries to buy new books nor to employ more than a few librarians full-time, and the uncertainty of its future funding has led to a loss of staff.

While the two are, in many ways, "sister" organizations, the museum is, unfortunately, much the poorer sister—fiscally, educationally and politically. The county museum is a smaller and much simpler institution than the county public library system, with our eleven libraries located in Roseburg and ten smaller cities and its dozens of employees. A great deal of time, expense and effort goes into tracking and handling the hundreds of thousands of books, compact disks and DVDs that our libraries offer.

The Douglas County Library system has a much broader, more complicated and more basic mission than the Museum of History and Natural History. We can go to the museum and pay a fee to learn about history and nature but the accumulated knowledge from every field of human inquiry is available, free of charge, at our public libraries.

I have often heard public libraries described as "bulwarks of democracy" but I've never heard anyone use that sort of language about museums. Our nation's free public libraries were founded expressly for the purpose of providing free open access to knowledge in the belief that an informed electorate protects us all.

Because our public library system is a much larger and more complex organization than the museum, it is critical that in any merger the overall direction must be in the hands of a fully qualified library director. Anything less, on that score, would, of course, be utterly unacceptable. That said, the same question arises in regard to the museum. Would a qualified library system director be qualified to run the museum?

Does merging these two programs improve the outlook for the library system? Our goal is to obtain adequate and sustainable funding for our public library system. We can see no way of achieving that goal without the passage of a countywide library service district measure. It is inevitable if we are to save this wonderful institution without cannibalizing some of our branch libraries to feed the others.

Having suffered an unsuccessful attempt to place a library service district measure on the ballot we are naturally leery of supplying those who opposed the creation of a service district with yet another reason to reject it in the future. We fear that there will be those who will suggest that while they might support the library if it stands alone, they will not want to support the museum as well.

What will be the true savings of such a merger? How much cost, if any, would this action actually save the county? Obviously, we cannot say with certainty just what that might come to yet, as no one really knows just exactly what shape this merger would take. Nevertheless, we do see a few potential problems ahead.

A single director running both institutions would, unavoidably, be less effective at doing both of those jobs than having (as is current) one director position assigned to each institution. It would appear that in order to have a single director for both, you would need to create two assistant director positions, one for each institution, in order to solve this.

LIBRARIANS ARE WEEPING OVER ERODING COUNTY SYSTEM

These are times that try librarians' souls. I wish it weren't so. I wish that I didn't have to see these dedicated public servants weeping, but that's what I've run into three times in the past twelve months.

They hide it from the public, of course.

"We just keep smiling," one librarian told me, "No matter what comes, the important thing is to keep on smiling. I do my screaming in the car on the way home."

Those smiles, I suspect, are getting harder for our county library's staff to wear. Consider the state of things:

The Douglas County Library system has faced uncertain funding for years now. When Max Leek, the recently retired director of our public libraries, retired, he mentioned that when he hired on with the county twelve years ago, no one was sure if the money to run it would be there next year. Actually, the budget cuts began three years before Mr. Leek's arrival, in 1997, when we lost our Bookmobile rural community service.

Layoffs over the years have greatly reduced the size of the staff, often forcing those who remain to handle what used to be done by two people. Since virtually none of the staff is currently working full time, the eighty hours of work of two people is expected to be done by one person in thirty-five hours.

There is no county budget money to purchase those books, compact discs and digital video discs that are freely loaned out to the public. That money now comes solely from charitable donations.

Nor is there much in the way of money for staff training.

Our five larger libraries used to be open forty hours per week and the six smaller ones for thirty hours. They are now only open for twenty-four hours in the larger libraries and sixteen hours in the smaller libraries. That is, we are at about 60% of a full-time library system. During the first few months of 2011, those hours were set to be cut down to sixteen hours and twelve hours respectively—40% of a library system. Were it not for a timely and large bequest, that 40% level would have likely been the situation last year and this.

Last fall and early winter brought a library service district measure campaign which sought to bring the library system back up to 80% of the open-door hours but failed when the city councils in five of our county's twelve cities would not allow the people in their cities to vote on the issue. Of those five city councils only two, Elkton and Sutherlin, actually voted to not pass the resolution. Myrtle Creek's council voted to not vote on the resolution that would have allowed their citizens to vote, while Winston and Canyonville simply allowed the motion to die for lack of a second—not even voting to not vote. Thus, a small group of what amounted to roughly twenty people was able to prevent the entire county from deciding whether or not we, the people, want to provide adequate and stable funding for our libraries.

The library's Board of Directors are the county commissioners. It being a county department, all responsibility for the system's health lies entirely with Doug Robertson, Susan Morgan and Joe Laurence. For reasons that were never explained, they chose not to support last year's service district proposal.

There seems to be a mistaken belief among our

county's commissioners that our beloved library system is now being funded at an acceptable minimum level. If we define that minimum as a level of funding that does no harm, then the current level can only be seen as well below that minimum. The system is being steadily eroded, wearing away bit by bit as the collection deteriorates and as key staff go looking for steady full-time work elsewhere or retire and are not replaced.

Now the system's director has gone and there is talk about the doubtful benefits of some sort of consolidation of the library with another county department.

I don't wonder a bit about why librarians weep. It's a noble profession and a much nobler public service than holding political office. Librarians care about their work. It is not just a gig for them but something that they have very deep and strong emotions about. For them this must be like watching a beloved family member slowly and painfully passing away. And they must weep as well to see their life's vital work treated as if it were no more than a string of digits on a spreadsheet.

The News-Review 10/10/2012

By 2015 it was obvious that a new effort would have to be made and so the Library Futures Committee resumed planning for 2016.

DOUGLAS COUNTY LIBRARY SYSTEM NEEDS FUNDING

Our Douglas County Library System is probably the most popular of all the services that our local tax dollars provide. So, it is only natural that when a funding crisis comes along, people try to come up with solutions to help preserve the system. Unfortunately, the most common of these schemes either simply don't work or can't be applied.

One often-heard proposal is to charge fees for library cards. Actually, the DCLS does, in fact, charge a $50.00 fee for some library cards. But these are for people who don't live in the library district, that is, within our county. Oregon law prohibits tax-funded libraries from charging card fees to residents of their districts. This is because public libraries are either free libraries or they are not public libraries.

The Peterborough Public Library in Peterborough, New Hampshire was the first tax-supported free public library in the world back when it opened in 1833, and this is how we've done things here in America ever since. "We the people" provide ourselves with unlimited access to books, CDs, DVDs, magazines, newspapers, computers and children's programs and we do so at public expense. It is a compassionate act and a generous act—one that speaks well of us as a people.

I've heard it said that The U.S. Constitution, baseball and Jazz constitute the three great gifts of the

American people to the world. I would add the creation of free public-supported libraries to that short list.

Another common suggestion is to hand the running of our libraries over to a for-profit company. In some cases, this works out to be cheaper for the taxpayers because the company pays out considerably less in wages and benefits to library staff.

A few years back, the Douglas County Commissioners, in their role as Board of Directors for the library system, asked for an estimate from the outfit that runs Jackson County's public libraries. The private sector's studied answer was that they couldn't run our libraries any cheaper than the way it was already being done. For-profit enterprises, of course, need to make a profit and after several years of annual trimming there just wasn't enough fat left to make privatization profitable without closing the doors on some of our eleven libraries. The commissioners weren't willing to close any branches and so the notion was dropped.

This remarkable efficiency in a government institution does not come cheaply. There is a human and institutional cost to saving taxpayer dollars. At present, the doors of our libraries are open 40% fewer hours than they had traditionally been, a significant loss to the patrons. Our library system's staffing has been cut, forcing fewer people to do more work and to do so in less time. There are, at present, only six full-time employees and the system has been losing workers frequently as they abandon our county system for full-time employment elsewhere. And there are no county taxes spent on the collection itself. For years now, every new book on those shelves has been paid for with private charitable donations scraped together by the Friends of the Library, the Douglas County Library Foundation and bequests from kindly citizens.

It is difficult to get people to understand that the current level of funding (about $1.5 million per year) is neither adequate nor sustainable. The system is already in serious decline and has been for the past fifteen years and studies done by the Douglas County Library Foundation estimate that it would take about $3 million yearly to both adequately serve our county's residents and maintain a healthy library system.

The county commissioners have asked Harold Hayes, the library system's director, to prepare budget scenarios calling for a "hold the line" budget at the current level (which given the fact of inflation is itself a budget cut), and a budget based on a 25% cut below the current level. To meet this 25% cut, the system will be forced to either close some of our libraries or to reduce open-door hours drastically.

Given the inevitable (and long forewarned) loss of our "safety net" federal funding and the property tax limitation laws that were passed in the 1990s, we will undoubtedly be faced with a mix of specifically targeted tax ballot measures as well as increased usage fees to make up the shortfall. What services we choose to support and at what level will say a great deal about us as a people and determine just what sort of a future we'll have here.

The News-Review 3/25/2015

A draft of an unpublished column 5/27/15

HOW WE GOT IN THIS MESS: A BRIEF HISTORY

The Douglas County Public Library system was founded in 1955 at a time when the county's general fund was fat with federal timber sales money.

From 1950 until 1990, logging went on at the rate of 1 billion board feet per year in our county, one third of which came off of the 52% of the land that is in federal ownership. A law enacted in the 1930s reserves a portion of federal timber sales money for the use of counties in which the trees are sold and cut. Since the federal government pays no local property taxes it was decided that county governments should receive payments from the sale of federally owned timber in compensation. These payments amounted to about $40 to $50 million dollars per year and paid the lion's share of funding for our schools and our county's general fund and kept our local property taxes significantly lower than the statewide and national averages.

Following the listing of northern spotted owls on the Endangered Species list in 1990, logging on federal lands in our county declined rapidly during the 1990s, while the federal government faced lawsuits from environmental organizations and timber industry groups and our county government. By 2005, federal timber sales funding had dropped to about 10% of the pre-1990 levels.

The Douglas County Public Library system took its first budget cuts in 1997. Among other losses, we lost our system's Bookmobile, a van that served our most remote communities in this large and largely rural county. From

1997 through 2007, the funding remained relatively stable as a so-called "safety net" allocation of federal tax revenue became a substitute for timber sales receipts. The legislation authorizing these emergency payments has always been time-limited, requiring renewal every five years or so. The latest round of payments was set up to become smaller with each passing year in the hope of gradually reducing the county's dependence on the years-long temporary funding. We are now in the final year of the current "safety net" money cycle, a year in which the payments have been reduced by 35% from the previous year. Congress may or may not renew those payments this time around and, if they do agree to another four or five years of payments, those will be smaller yet than the already shrunken funds.

As the "safety net" has shrunk, our public library system has shrunk along with it. During the first three years of cuts, the system managed to keep the doors of our eleven public libraries open for virtually the same number of hours while their funding dropped from $2.1 million in 2007 to $1.7 million in 2010. For the most part, this was accomplished by laying off employees, putting off capital improvements and buying fewer books and publications.

The 2011 county budget has brought "the unkindest cut of all"—a 21% cut leaving our public library system with $1.46 million in funding, greatly reduced hours of operation and a significantly smaller staff. As a result of this series of deceasing budgets, our public library system has been reduced to the point where the needs of our families, friends and neighbors can no longer be met.

Resuming my role as "Media Contact Guy," this time for the Save Our Libraries Political Action Committee for the second tax-base campaign.

MAKING SURE THE LIBRARY SYSTEM SURVIVES

People are surprised when I tell them that the board of directors for our county library system keeps cutting its annual budget while having no workable plan to ever provide adequate and sustainable funding. They become less surprised when I tell them that our county commissioners are also the library system's board.

It does seem odd that the people who are charged with looking after the wellbeing of our county's best-loved service can't bring themselves to actually support it. However, the commission is made up of politicians and we do live in a county where anti-taxation sentiment runs high—thus a reluctance to do what it takes to keep the doors open.

For some of our neighbors this "taxed enough already" attitude is the result of sincerely held ideological beliefs. But for most, I think, it is a matter of fear, resentment and distrust. We fear ever-increasing taxation; we resent government waste; we distrust our leaders. All of which is understandable. As a result, our leaders fear us, and this too is understandable.

If we are to preserve public access to all of the great good that our libraries bring us, it will require us to be courageous. Fear, of course, is natural and universal—all of us are sometimes fearful. Courage, though, is a matter of not allowing your fear to keep you from performing your duty.

It is our duty as Umpquans and as Americans to

provide each other with a functioning library system. For well over one hundred and eighty years now, communities in the United States (and later, thanks to America's example, around the globe) have used local tax dollars to create and support free public libraries.

Why? Out of humane kindness and human decency, to begin with, but also because our public libraries go a long way toward keeping "the domestic tranquility" more tranquil in so many ways. Your local library is both a temple of knowledge and a temple of compassion. It is an institution that we can all be proud to support, one that is open, democratic and (given the price-tag) a remarkably cheap way to keep our communities livable and our property values higher.

Yes, for those of us who need a personal reason to cough up a few bucks beyond being a library user or simply "for the good of all," it is worth considering that having a free public library increases property values, while not having them makes a place less desirable for families and therefore less valuable on the real estate market. Even a small one or two percent drop in home values can quickly cost a homeowner more money than the cost of two decades-worth of library services.

There is now an effort being made to take control of the Douglas County Library System away from the county commissioners and to place it in the hands of an independent board of directors elected by the people of our county. The commissioners have presided over the decline and what is likely to be eventual destruction of this essential service for decades now. But, beyond a few inane and unworkable suggestions, they really have no ideas about how to save the system. Given the current state of the county's budget, it should come as a relief to the commissioners to have our libraries paid for by an independent levy, thus freeing up funds for other uses.

Members of the Save Our Libraries Political Action Committee are currently asking city councils throughout the county to allow their citizens to vote on a ballot measure next November which would provide adequate and sustainable funding for what really is one of the best things we can do for each other. Should the measure pass (and there's no guarantee of that) those cities that do not participate in the vote will find their citizens excluded from the new special district and unable to borrow books without paying a substantial annual fee for a library card that would otherwise be free.

The Umpqua country is all one watershed, and we are all one people. Whether or not we can come together and do some good for ourselves and each other by making sure our library system survives and that open-door hours are at least partially restored remains to be seen. We do, at the very least, deserve the chance to try it, with or without the support of our elected officials.

The News-Review 2/18/16

Early in the 2016 effort, the Save Our Libraries PAC spent two or three weeks gathering signatures on a petition to the county Board of Commissioners asking that they allow the library support measure to be placed on the county ballot. The petition drive ended when the board finally said that they would allow it providing that "enough cities" would put it on their city ballots. The role of The Cat was played in costume by Rita Radford, the Assistant Librarian of Riddle's library.

JOURNAL ENTRY: ADVENTURES IN PETITIONING 3/4/2016

I've been standing out in public often lately while gathering signatures for our library district measure and it is encouraging to meet so many kind-hearted people and amusing at times to meet some of the not-so-kindly disposed.

So far, I've gathered 235 signatures and only one person has actually come out against the existence of public libraries. "I don't approve of libraries," he said, "They let the kids in there and they make a mess, and they let them see things they shouldn't see and besides, they aren't government run—they're run by a private business." All of which, of course, is patently false except that they really do let kids in there.

Monday was Dr. Seuss Day at the Myrtle Creek Public Library, an annual affair. About a dozen parents and thirty children, mostly pre-school age, came to meet The Cat in The Hat and hear a story and to go fishing for trinkets in the Red Fish, Blue Fish little cardboard booth. I stood outside the door collecting signatures and watching the show through the windows and recalling all of the folks who have told me over the years that "No one uses the library anymore."

It was time, once again, to ask the county commissioners to support our library district proposal. For my part, I chose to speak with commissioner Susan Morgan, a fellow Myrtle Creek resident with whom I had served for a time on our local Library Advisory Board before she went into politics. She refused to endorse the measure but promised not to oppose it.

LETTER TO COMMISSIONER MORGAN

9 May 2016

Dear Susan,

Here is my post-mortem analysis of the December 2011 library support poll done by TMS for the Save Our Libraries PAC. The polling information arrived shortly after we had to abandon the effort and I went through the stats to see how the public opinion around the county differed from place to place and, in particular, what the voters in each of the cities that adopted or rejected the resolution actually wanted. With that in mind, I focused on only three of the questions asked.

As you will see, with a 48% countywide support base and 36% opposition with 16% remaining undecided, the measure would most likely have passed, since the opposition would have needed to come up with 94% (15 of 16 points) of the undecided voters to defeat it while the PAC needed only 19% (3 of 16 points) of them for victory. By the way, our library measure consultants, Every Library, tell us that the national average on an initial library measure polling outcome runs along the lines of 37% for, 37% against and 26% undecided.

One of the sad aspects of politics is that part of me worries about handing this information over to you. The fear is that doing so might bring harm to the effort somehow—this, even though we two have known each other for decades now and have worked together a few times in the past. It is an irrational fear, of course, and I recognize it as such. Well, I suppose this wariness toward you is mostly due to the way things came down the last time we came around with a proposal and reflects much more on your position itself than on your character.

From our extensive studies of other library district measures here in Oregon, we know that the endorsement of the local county commissioners makes this sort of measure much more likely to pass, while the refusal to endorse by, or the opposition of, commissioners make them much more likely to fail. As such, even a purely neutral position can seem to amount to a sort of passive-aggressive opposition. This too, I guess, is a source of irrational distrust on my part.

The form of the current effort, in establishing an independent special district, came about because we, as a group, felt that we could not trust our commissioners, and therefore needed to take the system away from county government control. Nevertheless, when I polled our PAC about whether to share this old polling information with you, the group OK'd it unanimously.

There is an old Alsatian proverb of my ancestors which tells me that, "To trust everyone is foolish; to trust no one is insane." So, if we have erred in trusting too much, at least we have the comfort of doing so foolishly, rather than insanely.

We will be conducting a new poll soon and those results will give us a more accurate picture of local attitudes toward paying taxes to support a countywide public library system.

Peace,

Bob Heilman
(541) xxx-xxxx
xxxxxxxxx@frontier.com

AS OTHERS SEE US

I've been telling friends of mine from Lane County about how it is that we may lose our Douglas County Library System altogether as early next January. Their reactions have been interesting.

At first, they are, of course, appalled by the notion that public libraries could ever be closed for lack of funding. After all, this is the United States of America, and we are the people who invented free public libraries. Towns and cities here have libraries, lots of them—more public libraries than McDonalds has burger joints in this country. All of us have grown up with and in them. The notion seems surreal. It's like trying to tell people that a week after Christmas the moon will no longer rise, or that, come January, all the world's fish will be gone forever.

I do point out to them that we will be having a vote on the November election ballot to raise a little tax money to keep them open. Unfortunately, I can't tell them whether or not that measure will pass or if, instead, we'll be kissing all eleven of our libraries goodbye soon after.

Once the shock wears off, my Emerald Empire friends fall back on an attitude that they've had for a very long time: "How can you stand to live there?" they ask.

"Well, it's my home," I tell them while wondering why they don't realize just how rude and insensitive that question is.

Most of what they find distasteful about Douglas County is really due to their liberal disdain for our conservative voters, whom they characterize as "a bunch of ignorant rednecks." (This bigoted image, by the way, was reinforced heavily last fall when armed lunatic fringe protestors descended on Roseburg to protest President Obama's brief personal visit in the wake of the UCC massacre.) It simply rankles them that we generally vote 2–1 for Republican candidates while they vote 2–1 for Democrats.

Well, it is true that Lane County people look down on us here in the One Hundred Valleys and don't want to live here. After all, the company formerly known as Roseburg Lumber is moving its corporate headquarters soon to Lane County for that very reason.

And who will want to live here after we have shut down our libraries? Not much of anybody, I fear. Certainly, it will be impossible to persuade any large-scale employers to settle here, in a place where their managers' children have no public library to go to. Do we really need to reinforce our neighboring county's negative stereotypes about who we are? I can't think of a better way to convince our urban neighbors to the north that we are indeed a bunch of worthless yahoos down here.

Nevertheless, our county commissioners have apparently arranged this year's library budget in such a way that, following the latest and most brutal in a long series of annual budget cuts, there will be almost nothing left on January 1st, 2017. According to Commissioner Chris Boice, the library system's liaison on the board, what remains after the first day of next year will amount to "a few hundred thousand dollars"—just enough to close it all down.

The Douglas County Board of Commissioners has recently placed the ballot measure on November's ballot. So, we will all have a chance to vote on it. Whether it passes or not will say much to the world at large—and to ourselves as well—about who we really are.

The News-Review 6/24/2016

MEMOS

In seeking support for the 2016 tax-base measure, we contacted various groups around the county. A small group of us did meet with The News-Review *editorial board and convinced them to support the effort. The paper's lead reporter, Carisa Cevgaske, sent me the following queries in preparing a series of feature articles which appeared on 10/16/16, 10/18/16 and 11/3/16.*

Query Response #1

Q1

The PAC comes out of the Library Futures Committee of the Douglas County Library Foundation. Back in 2003 the Foundation recognized the necessity of finding adequate and sustainable funding for the library system. After studying the matter, it was decided that creating a tax base was the best solution. At the request of the county commissioners, the effort was put on hold due to concerns about O&C and Forest Service timber payments. In 2010 the Library Futures Committee became active again and in September of 2011 members of the Futures Committee formed the Save Our Libraries PAC.

The SOL PAC tried and failed to get a special district measure on the ballot.

In 2015 it became obvious that the county would soon be forced to abandon the library system, and the PAC regrouped. A small core group spent months creating an Economic Feasibility Study and by January 2016 began work on getting the measure approved by Douglas County's twelve cities. Ten cities signed on with Sutherlin and Elkton absenting.

The group is diverse, about a dozen people or so

at its core. We have a balance of men and women, and it includes people who are registered to vote as Democrats, Republicans and Non-affiliated. It is a very talented group which is composed almost entirely of retirees. So, we've got a retired judge, a retired college art instructor, a retired public relations firm executive, a former fireman, a retired U.S. Coast Guardsman, a retired business consultant, a former bookstore owner, a former librarian and yours truly, a hippie from Myrtle Creek.

What brings us together is a shared love of books and of libraries.

Q2

Well, actually, what with the loss of Sutherlin it will be more like $3.8 million. The library system's budget back in the mid-1990s was running about $3.4 million in CPI-indexed 2016 dollars. The library budget of $2.8 million in 2008, upon which our plan was built comes to $3.2 million in CPI-indexed 2016 dollars.

The 2008 library system budget was already one that had been cut a few times going back to 1996, when we lost Bookmobile service in this county. As such the 2008 budget left the library system at a minimally functional level as rated by the Oregon State Library (or Oregon Library Association?). In part, this low rating is due to the failure of the county government to supply materials for the collection since 2008—book not, neither CD, DVD nor magazine subscription. The cutbacks in hours due to the 10% cut in 2009, the 10% cut in 2010, the 10% cut in 2011 haven't helped much either.

In setting both the tax rate and the level of desired service, there were two primary criteria: adequacy and sustainability. Does it meet the needs? Can it survive to continue meeting that need? The secondary goal was to do so as cheaply as possible in order to keep the tax rate as low as we could while still meeting the primary goal. We are convinced that it can't be done cheaper.

The added cost of running the system, roughly $0.6 million, comes from added expense of not being a county agency and therefore able to use county services such as Legal, HR, IT and PERS as well the need to build a reserve that is capable of meeting emergency expenses. Also, should the measure pass, Roseburg will no longer be paying the county $50,000 a year toward upkeep of the Roseburg Headquarters Library, a cost to be assumed by the new district.

Should the measure pass: It will restore open-door hours (e.g. Roseburg from 24 hours per week to 45); It will provide for keeping the collection up to date; it will create jobs; it will take the control over the library system away from the county commissioners and put it in the hands of five people, elected at large, who love libraries.

Q3

Six people are running for five positions: Joe Coyne, Reedsport; Norm Gershon, Roseburg; Bob Bell, Winston; Jim Williams, Roseburg; Carol Hilderbrand, Days Creek.

Norm and Carol are not members of the SOL PAC, the rest are. Carol is a retired librarian (Canyonville Branch Library).

Q4

Current employees would be employed (or laid off) by the county government until July 1st, 2017. The new district would then likely offer them continued employment. ("Likely," because at this point, with no

Board and an election pending no one can speak on behalf of what is not yet in existence.)

Q5

Employment will be equal to 45.6 Full Time Employment (FTE) positions.

Q6

Only the Roseburg Headquarters Library belongs to the county. All others belong to their respective cities and are staffed and supplied and serviced under inter-governmental agreements. The cities provide the building and maintenance, and the county supplies the libraries.

As for Q's 7-12, give me a call and we'll talk about those. The ballgame's on and it is do-or-die for my Dodgers.

Peace,

Bob Heilman
541-xxx-xxxx

Query Response #2
Q7
No, they are keeping up with and providing electronically delivered information and entertainment. Library to Go provides downloads of e-books and the computer stations in all of our libraries and are busy. You cannot digitize preschool storytime nor the Summer Reading Program nor the kindness of a librarian in listening respectfully to a lonely senior citizen.

Immanuel Kant, the philosopher, distinguished two forms of value, instrumental value and intrinsic value. It is a mistake to think of libraries only in terms of their great instrumental value, as a tool, like a screwdriver, to be valued only for their immediate personal utility. Libraries have intrinsic value as well, that is, they have value in their own right as working examples of the goodness of collective generosity and as integral parts of our American cultural identity. They are an important part of who we are, keeping "urbanity, culture and beauty for its own sake from passing away."

There are no solid stats on the number of library users that I'm aware of, but rather stats on usage (i.e.. the number of borrowings but not the number of borrowers.) There are stats on the number of library card holders, but these have recently become a matter of controversy, due to a change in tracking card use instituted by Chris Boice. Traditionally, libraries have calculated the number of card holders by usage within the past three years. Boice, in an effort to generate $12 donations to help offset operational costs, has instituted an annual card renewal regimen. The difference in the two methods—one year vs. three-years—yields a large gap, in the thousands, as to how many valid card holders are listed. Harold Hayes could supply the actual figures.

Q8

To outsiders, we will look like a bunch of ignorant tight-fisted yahoos, an opinion that many outside our county already share. Without libraries I would expect our already high adult functional illiteracy rate to increase and our already high school dropout rate to go up as well. As a result of those factors and an increased difficulty in business recruiting due to the loss of our library system, poverty and crime rates will likely go up as well.

Q9

What is touted as "Plan B" is a haphazard collection of mostly inane suggestions for running libraries without funding or librarians—putting a Starbucks in the lobby is one of my favorite unworkable ideas. This "alternative" notion uses the Josephine County model which provides their patrons with the least viable and least useful library service in Southern Oregon. Their library system, like ours as it currently is, does not provide adequate services and is not sustainable. Their operational plan specifically calls for establishing their district as a Library Special District with a dedicated tax base (just like 10-145 proposes for us). DCLS ranks fifth of six Southern Oregon Counties in level of service to the patrons and failure of the measure would leave our system ranking sixth.

An immediate concern is that, even should the measure pass, the county has only budgeted roughly three months' worth of funding to last from January 1st to June 30th, roughly $400,000. While that is enough to shut down the system, it is not enough to keep all the branches open. Mr. Boice seems to believe that the shortfall will be made up by charitable donations, but there is no evidence that such funds are available from any source.

In short, what is currently being touted as a viable alternative is not something that would be considered as a sound business plan by any reputable business consultant or bank loan officer.

Q10

Myrtle Creek city councilor Gail Black is the council representative on the Myrtle Creek Public Library Citizen Advisory Board. At our September meeting she said that the city would not be able to run a library on its own given the state of the town's finances. Myrtle Creek is one of the larger municipalities in our county and the towns where the smaller library branches are located—Glendale, Canyonville, Riddle, Oakland, Yoncalla and Drain—would have an even tougher time of it financially.

Establishing a town library is a complicated process that raises many questions. Would it have a tax base? What would be the boundaries for the single-town system—the city limits or the zip code? It would require another ballot measure, local this time, presumably in May 2017. However, the groundwork for that would have to be completed within a matter of four months or so after the November 8th, 2016 election in order to be placed on the ballot. If that election is missed then it would have to be a vote later on down the line, during which there would be no funding. The city would find itself trying to reopen its library after a months-long shutdown. If such a vote passes there would still be a lag time between the election and the point at which taxes could be collected. This period could run as long as a full year.

The whole process is fraught with uncertainty and difficulties.

Q11

"Privatization" of libraries carries two meanings. The first, and most common, is that of running a public library as a for-profit business, in essence, as a book and video rental store or subscription library. Oregon State law prohibits public libraries from charging their patrons fees to use the library. All public libraries in Oregon are free public libraries. Charging for library cards, requiring a subscription or renting out materials from the collection would result in a loss of nonprofit status, leaving that library unable to obtain grants, donations and bequests that help keep costs down and services up.

The second sort of privatization would be to retain nonprofit status and turn over the operation of the library to a for-profit library management company. Jackson County's library system has contracted with Library Systems and Services Incorporated for that purpose. This outfit achieves cheaper costs and profits for its investors by paying lower wages than what government-run libraries pay, with lower benefits chiefly by avoiding having to pay Public Employee Retirement benefits. This is something the newly elected board can and likely will consider doing. However, the Jackson County Library System's Board of Directors is having buyer's remorse. (See: *Mail-Tribune* editorial.)

Q12

To begin with, compression is the law of the land in

Oregon and, fair or unfair, there's nothing that our PAC can do about that. Compression is common in Roseburg, Winston and Reedsport but not universal. Tim Freeman, for example, has three property tax bills all of which are in compression, so, for him, his personal tax increase would be $0.00, rather than the $400 increase that he has claimed (were it not in compression his tax increase would actually come to $310 per year); Gary Leif has four property tax bills, two of which are in compression and two which are not, so, his taxes would go up by $208 per year rather than the $600 increase that he has claimed; Chris Boice's property, located in rural Myrtle Creek, is not in compression and his tax bill would go up by $158 per year.

Because the true effect of compression can only be calculated by examining every single tax bill one-by-one, no one has been able to come up with a verifiable dollar amount as to how it will affect any particular tax rate. The PAC's closest estimate for Roseburg's overall property taxes runs from a low of $300,000 to a high of $600,000, an unavoidably broad range.

Compression affects all of the tax-supported services equally, including measure 10-145's $0.44 per $1,000 of assessed value. Thus, property owners in compression would be paying something along the lines of maybe $0.38 per $1,000 toward the libraries. It is a matter of choosing which services are to be funded out of the $10 limit. Should those 38 pennies go to city or county government? Should some part of those $10 be dedicated to preserving our libraries? The voters must choose.

MEDIA ADVISORY

Re: Douglas County Library Measure 10-145 Kick-off Event 9/20/16

The Save Our Libraries Political Action Committee will be kicking off its Library Special District Measure campaign with an event to be held on Tuesday, September 20th from 11am to 12 noon in the Ford Community Room at the Douglas County Library System's headquarters library located at 1409 NE Diamond Lake Blvd. in Roseburg, Oregon.

The measure seeks to keep the county's public libraries in operation by establishing the library system as an independent property-tax-supported institution with a tax base of $0.44 per thousand dollars of assessed value. The system is currently run by the county government and the county government will no longer fund any of the eleven libraries in its countywide system. It is expected that the closure process for the libraries will begin in January 2017 and be completed by June 30, 2017, if the measure fails to pass.

Communities affected by the library closure are Glendale, Canyonville, Riddle, Myrtle Creek, Winston, Roseburg, Sutherlin, Oakland, Yoncalla, Drain and Reedsport.

Attached is an FAQ sheet regarding the measure and a link to the SOL PAC website. For further information or interview requests please contact:

Robert Leo Heilman
541-xxx-xxxx
xxxxxxxxx@frontier.com

"PLAN B" FOR OUR LIBRARIES

At the Spring Fair this year a man walked past the Save Our Libraries PAC booth and barked out, "Privatize it," and then kept walking away before I had a chance to ask him what, exactly, he meant by that somewhat ambiguous suggestion. Clearly, he somehow felt threatened, and I suppose he likely assumed that talking to one of his neighbors about something that concerned them both was a fruitless proposition. Luckily, most people, I have found, are willing to ask questions and to listen to the answers. They might disagree but at least they do try to understand, which is all it takes to be an informed citizen.

One of the more common questions that come up about the ballot measure that will establish a new adequate and sustainable countywide library district, is "What happens if the measure doesn't pass?" The truth is, no one knows for certain and so we can only talk about likely outcomes.

We know that the county commissioners have announced that they will no longer fund the current library system. What is likely is that library service in Douglas County will become chaotic and irregular with our towns left on their own if they want to provide adequate library services to their citizenry. Some towns will, no doubt, try an experiment to see whether it is possible to sustainably run a library without a librarian or funding. A few may actually form viable small library districts for themselves—a difficult and lengthy process requiring much research, many meetings and some sort of reasonably steady funding from the city.

If the suggestions that have surfaced so far as

possible alternatives to a countywide integrated library system are any indication, those who want to rely on a vaguely defined "Plan B" have not done their homework.

The fellow who wanted to privatize our libraries probably wanted to have them become for-profit businesses, rather than remaining non-profit educational institutions. Oregon law provides that all public libraries must be free public libraries. A privatized library, in this sense of the word, is no longer public but a sort of privately operated rental business, ineligible for grants or charitable donations or bequests and denying access to anyone who can't cough up the money on demand.

Perhaps the most glaring failure of understanding among the proponents of a vague and improbably cheaper way to provide adequate and sustainable libraries is that there really are such things as economies of scale. Ten libraries formed into a district are simply cheaper to run than ten individual libraries because they can split many of the costs among themselves with no need to duplicate essentials such as Payroll, Human Resources, Internet Technology and Cataloging duties in every town. The cheaper operating cost is a benefit to taxpayers and having access to a larger shared collection is another benefit. After all, more selection and lower costs is generally seen as a good thing when compared to the alternative of paying more for less.

What those who believe in the sketchy notion of alternative ways of providing library services are proposing is a haphazard set of individual city-run libraries without the funding and expertise necessary to meet accepted standards.

Yes, free public libraries, just like schools, need to meet basic standards such as having qualified staffing, funds to keep up the collection and having enough open-door hours to meet the need of their patrons. Measure 10-145 meets those standards and will allow the Douglas County Library System to carry on into the future. It can do so with a simple "Yes" vote and an eminently reasonable property tax rate of forty-four pennies per thousand dollars-worth of assessed value.

    The real alternative is to choose a complicated and expensive route to a doubtful future.

The News-Review 10/6/2016

I prepared two speeches for election night, November 8th, 2016.

DEFEAT STATEMENT DRAFT:

Tonight's defeat of county Measure 10-145 saddens us, but it does not discourage us. Our striving to provide adequate and sustainable library services to the people of Douglas County has been an ongoing effort for many years now and we fully intend to keep that effort going. While the future of our county's library system is now in greater doubt than ever, we do not doubt that preserving access to our free public libraries is essential to having a brighter and more fruitful future for our beloved home here in these Umpqua Valleys.

The hard work of over one thousand supporters, campaign donors and volunteers has not been in vain. Tens of thousands of our neighbors have been reminded of the incalculable value of their public libraries and made aware of their libraries' dire state on the verge of passing away. Our faith has always been in the people of Douglas County and that has not changed. We look forward to working with all of our neighbors to provide libraries that meet the public's need, and which will have the ability to keep meeting those needs on into the future.

VICTORY STATEMENT DRAFT:

Naturally, tonight's passage of county Measure 10-145 pleases us. Yet it is not, in any real sense, our victory but one that belongs to our neighbors, tens of thousands of whom have shown that they recognize the important role of our free public libraries in making life better for all of us. We ourselves could not have done this alone, without the hard work of over one thousand supporters, campaign donors and volunteers. It is their victory, and we thank them for responding to the challenge and working to ensure that our free public libraries will continue to be there for us as we reach for a brighter and more fruitful future together.

Tonight, we celebrate but with the sober knowledge that thi is only a brief pause in our efforts. Much work remains to be done in establishing this new library district. Its newly elected board of directors will need everyone's full support if we are to come through the difficult and complicated transition from being a county government agency to creating an independent service district.

For tonight, we shall rest from our labors—for tomorrow the work begins again.

ON BEARING BAD NEWS

The worst of it all was going back to the party from the courthouse on election eve with the result in hand. At least, while walking the few dark blocks to the courthouse with two other political action committee members I wasn't alone and, in those minutes, there was still some hope.

La esperanza muere última, it is said: "Hope dies last." This is probably an ancient proverb, no doubt expressed somewhere in the writings of a Seneca or a Cicero and, if so, even way back then, it would probably have been a thought lifted from older sources. Human nature, after all, hasn't changed perceptibly since writing was invented and before that happy innovation we have no record.

The news was bad.

We had lost in the election by a margin of forty-four percent to fifty-six percent. As a result, all eleven public libraries in our county would have to be shut down, perhaps never to reopen.

The election night party at the restaurant was full of people who had worked very hard to get tax-base funding for what was once one of the finest library systems in Oregon. I knew it was over, but they didn't know that yet and it was my duty to inform them.

A few minutes before leaving the courthouse I'd been handed a printout listing the election results. I had just enough time to read it, mutter "Damn!" and glance up at the editor of our small local right-wing weekly newspaper and note his smug grin before the local daily's lead reporter held her recorder up to my face and asked for a statement.

This too was my duty.

A few days before the election I had written two formal statements for others to use—one magnanimous in victory, the other courageous in defeat. I hadn't thought that I'd be called upon to speak for the Save Our Libraries campaign but those whom I'd written it for weren't there. "Naturally, we are disappointed by the results, but we are not discouraged…" I began.

While walking back down Roseburg's Main St. and trying my best to hold grief at bay long enough to do what was required of me, my thoughts ran back to ancient times—Alexandria burning, Goths at the gates of Rome. Sometimes it is best to focus on your anger and resentment, if that gets you through. It was better, for a time at least, to rage against the loss, than to think about the damage that would inevitably follow. These barbarians, I thought bitterly, were not menacing at the gates now but had entered our cities and being modern barbarians, they weren't burning the libraries, merely "defunding" them.

And I had failed to prevent it.

It is easier to accept defeat when there are others to blame, or to hate perhaps. Certainly, some of the anti-tax crowd's statements against funding libraries with property taxes were vile and disgusting falsehoods. But then, I had anticipated that a great deal of noisome mud would be flung in the final weeks before the election. The disciples of Grover Norquist stick to tried and true methods. They always come in late and hit hard during the last few weeks before an election when there's not enough time left to respond effectively. This is one of the things that make it easier to get people to vote "No" than to convince people to vote "Yes."

Fear though is what drives an anti-taxation campaign, both the deliberate instilling of fear as a campaign tactic and the simple existence of fear as a pervasive force within our national culture. As bitter as I was on that night (and I was as bitter as the waters of The Apocalypse), I knew that my neighbors were not against libraries. Their vote was, I knew, compounded of rejection of our government itself and an embracing of the fear of being "taxed to death." Unkind of me though it was, the phrase "fear-crazed tightwads" had struck me as an apt description of the opposition during the months leading up to the election.

Sometimes I think that the most radical thing an American can say is, "Don't be afraid."

The fear of the voters was mirrored within our library system but there it was a quieter fear, marked by the weeping of librarians. It is, I assure you, a very sad thing to hug teary-eyed librarians and sadder still to feel helpless while doing so.

Several years had passed, bringing ever-dwindling funds, yearly reduced hours of service and yet more staff layoffs until, by election night 2016, what was left of the countywide library system hadn't met anyone's standards of adequacy for eight consecutive years. "It's never open," had become an occasional argument for closing it all down.

Those who care about public libraries tend to care very deeply about them. At the county fair a woman came up to our booth and very nearly burst into tears talking about how important those libraries are to the poor folks whom she served.

"Libraries
The He♥rt
Of Every
Community,"
reads a lapel button that I wore all summer. If so, it seemed, we would shortly become a heartless community.

I tried not to think about the kids as I walked, but of course it was unavoidable. Preschool Storytime, Summer Reading, student homework sessions on the computers and librarians visiting the schools to promote literacy—all of it gone.

There really wasn't any time to process the loss in those few blocks of walking alone toward what I knew would be a room full of shocked and dismayed neighbors and friends. I found myself repeating a hopeless mantra, "Well, it's finally over now. It's all over now. It's over…" Except, of course, it wasn't over—at least not yet for me or for those thirty library supporters awaiting the news.

A television news reporter from Eugene stood on the sidewalk outside the restaurant with his camera mounted on its tripod. I wanted to breeze past him but courtesy and a sense of duty made me pause long enough to tell him the results. He asked to interview me after I'd told him the results.

"Not now," I told him, "I need to get inside and tell everyone what happened."

I'd managed to talk to two reporters without breaking down emotionally. This was very professional of me, I felt, as I headed for the backroom that we'd reserved in hope and would leave in despair.

A still photographer from the local daily and our local television news reporter had both come to the party while I was gone. Everyone looked up at me as I held up the printout and gave them the sad news.

"We have lost," I said, "fifty-six to forty-four percent. The numbers aren't likely to change much. It's all over."

I sat back down at my place at the table to stunned silence.

The lights went up for the TV camera and I soon heard my words being spoken by the president of the library foundation. There was an odd satisfaction in hearing the little concession speech that I'd crafted serving its purpose—to provide sure words to someone who'd been struck speechless moments before.

The room emptied pretty quickly after that, until only myself and my friend Karen remained. I'd promised to give the news director at a local radio station an election night interview and we waited there among the vacant tables and chairs until he called. Then Karen and I walked out together, back to our rides.

"I really thought we would win," Karen told me.

"I figured that we'd lose," I lied to her.

Oregon Humanities, Beyond the Margins, Portland OR 11/17/2017

Following the defeat of the library support measure on November 8, 2016, a public meeting was held in the Ford Family Room of the DCLS headquarters building in Roseburg on the evening of November 23, 2016. The meeting was chaired by county commissioner and DCLS liaison Chris Boice, an advocate of running the libraries on a volunteer basis with neither a tax base nor county funding. At the meeting it was revealed that the Douglas County Republican Party had contributed $1,500 to a private citizen for purchasing yard signs opposing both the library measure and a school district bond measure. It was also announced that a task force would form to study the question of what to do with the library system's collection.

Epilogue

The DCLS branch libraries all closed on April 1st, 2017, leaving only the headquarters building in Roseburg open and no longer providing library service to the public. A skeleton crew there handled the system's closing duties until the final closure of the system on June 30th, 2017.

In January of 2017, I joined the Board of Directors for the Douglas County Library Foundation, a post I held for two three-year terms from 2017–2023. At my first DCLF board meeting, county commissioner Chris Boice asked the foundation's board to use the remainder of the DCLF endowment to finance an extra year of funding for the county library system. The board voted unanimously against the proposal, which would have fully depleted the endowment fund balance.

The foundation has been growing those investment funds since 2017 and has been providing from $50,000 to $100,000 from its earnings in annual grants distributed among all of the county's eleven libraries.

Three of the original eleven county system's public libraries eventually formed their own smaller library districts, headquartered in Drain, Reedsport and Roseburg, three cities that voted for the 2016 property tax measure. Drain and Reedsport formed independent library districts. The library in Roseburg, the county seat and largest city in the county (population 23,690), reopened in 2019 with city budget funding after being closed for more than a year and a half. The three of them combined are serving about thirty percent of the county population.

The remaining libraries, in Canyonville, Glendale, Myrtle Creek, Oakland, Sutherlin, Riddle, Winston and Yoncalla, are all doing their best to serve the remaining seventy percent of the county's population. Lacking any tax base, they are operating on greatly reduced open-door hours and are depending on grants and charity to pay the bills and on the efforts of volunteers to do the work that used to be done by professionals. Most of these community libraries are struggling to survive and, lacking both tax bases and professional librarians, do not qualify as public libraries and are therefore ineligible for state support. In short, they are all better than nothing but still inadequate and in the long run, perhaps unsustainable.

The promised task force meetings occurred in the spring of 2017. The only useful outcome was that the county's eight volunteer-run community libraries formed the Douglas Community Library Association in the fall of 2017, a mutual assistance coalition of eight of the former DCLS branch libraries which serves to help recreate some of the old county system's benefits. I was a founding board member of the DCLA and served with them for two years, 2017–2019. The DCLA helps with inter-library materials loans through a shared catalog and collection management software system, honors their member libraries' cards, manages the Dolly Parton Imagination Library program for all eight libraries and provides some e-book access on a limited basis. Obtaining grants for the DCLA has been hampered in some instances by it lacking status as a library.

Overall, the combined library service from all eleven libraries in Douglas County is providing about 50% of the open-door hours of operation compared to what the DCLS traditionally had.

In Myrtle Creek the Friends of Myrtle Creek Library launched an effort to reopen the library. At this time, Douglas Education Service District wanted to lease the library building from the city as South County office space, offering to allow the use of the current Children's Room and the Periodicals Room (roughly 30% of the floor space) as library space to be staffed by ESD employees during business hours.

DRAFT LETTER AGAINST LEASING THE BUILDING 2/28/2017

FRIENDS OF THE MYRTLE CREEK LIBRARY
P.O. Box 499
Myrtle Creek, OR 97457
(541) xxx-xxxx
friendsofthemyrtlecreeklibrary@gmail.com

Summary:

A group of local citizens has formed for the purpose of maintaining a library and public space in our community. The group has received commitments from a reasonably large number of volunteers who are willing to provide staffing and funding for that purpose. Without this effort, the City of Myrtle Creek, as well as the surrounding community, will likely suffer the loss of their library. Such a loss would leave us all poorer and would preclude ongoing efforts to provide adequate library services to the community.

Current Efforts:

This proposal serves as an alternative to an imminent possibility that the Myrtle Creek Public Library building may be leased to a party that would not be committed to providing many of the services that are available in a well-run public library. It is unlikely that leasing the building to an institution whose primary goal is not to provide library services would result in a Summer Reading Program for children, outreach to local preschools and elementary schools to encourage literacy, a weekly Storytime reading, encouragement to parents to read to their children and, importantly, availability of books, CDs, DVDs to borrow at no cost to the patrons.

Such full (or, at least, more full-ranging) services

may be possible for the city to provide in the future if the fate of the library is left in the hands of a group dedicated to library services but would be nearly impossible to obtain otherwise.

There is an effort underway under a countywide Library Task Force to try to work out a way for libraries in various cities in Douglas County to provide a better system than any individual city would be capable of if operating alone. This Task Force's members have just begun their deliberations, and it is expected that their work will not be completed for several months yet. The Friends are willing to maintain at least a minimal level of service during and after the time this process works its way toward a conclusion. To lease the building out prior to completion of the Task Force process could make it impossible to enjoy the potential benefits of inter-city cooperation.

The Friends:

The Friends of the Myrtle Creek Library is a group of concerned citizens numbering about twenty individuals, many of whom have strong long-time records of active civic involvement. The group contains at its core the entire Myrtle Creek Public Library Citizens Advisory Board, a small group that has served the city well and faithfully for many years and whose members have a good deal of expertise in library matters. This library board is ready to guide the group by coordinating volunteer workers, overseeing fundraising and ensuring that this library functions efficiently, safely and legally.

The group is made up mostly—almost entirely, really—of retirees who are lovers of libraries. Within the group are members who have expertise in many useful fields such as public service, management, education and law.

Nuts and Bolts:

It is anticipated that the library would operate as a reading room at least temporarily, while the Library Task Force seeks their solution, and perhaps for some time afterward. The goal however, would be to ultimately return the library to the status of a fully functional public library, as defined under Oregon State law.

The library has raised money for itself over the years through efforts such as the bi-annual book sale, private donations and grants from charitable institutions. The library board currently has $xxxxxxx in funds already dedicated to supporting the library. This amount, by itself, is enough to easily provide public internet access via Wi-Fi for the building and to purchase the necessary computers for public use.

Many of the members of the Friends group have already committed to providing donations to support the effort if it goes forward. A good deal more could likely be raised rather quickly through a concerted effort along the lines of the City Swimming Pool's recent highly successful repair effort. Using those privately donated funds would make it possible to provide magazine and newspaper subscriptions and to pay for maintaining the computers and for necessary office supplies.

Library Advisory Board funds are currently accepted on behalf of the city and, at least for the first few months, would be funneled through the city. This would allow those who contribute to take a tax deduction, since donations to the city qualify due to its 501(c)-4 status. It may, or may not, become necessary for the Friends group to incorporate at a later date, depending on the outcome of the Task Force negotiations.

The Douglas County Library Foundation is willing to assist libraries in Douglas County by providing moderate funding to preserve library services. It is likely that similar grants will become available from the Ford Family Foundation.

We have received assurances that the county government will allow the city to keep the collection that is currently assigned to the Myrtle Creek Public Library.

By allowing the Friends' proposal to go forward, the city would, of course, still be able to adopt alternative plans as part of the 2017–2018 fiscal year budget process should that be found to be necessary.

Balancing Needs:

Leasing the building to a party whose primary purpose is not to provide a community library and safe space has but one advantage, that of providing income to the city. Dedicating the space to be used as a library would meet many needs and continue the original purpose of the building which was built using Federal Rural Library Program funds.

MYRTLE CREEK LIBRARY OUTCOME

The Friends of Myrtle Creek Library incorporated as a 501(C)3 nonprofit and convinced the city council by a vote of 3–2 to approve FOMCL taking over the library. The group signed contracts with the city to run and manage the library while the city agreed to provide the building, the utilities and maintenance of the building but not liability insurance. A separate contract was signed with the county government to allow FOMCL to own the collection as contained in the building.

On July 1st, 2017, Myrtle Creek Library reopened as the only lending library available in the county.* That same day saw the first session of the library's annual Summer Reading program. The FOMCL immediately began issuing free library cards to all county residents and tracking materials loans using the old-fashioned hand-written 3x5 card system for the first seven weeks of operation. In late August the Friends of Myrtle Creek Library signed with the Biblionix Apollo collection management software system which was later adopted by eight more libraries in the county. At the request of FOMCL, the computer software company developed interlibrary loan software which was eventually adopted and used by all of the county's eight Douglas Community Libraries Association libraries.

Because the city council of Sutherlin had refused, for the second time, to allow their citizens to vote on the 2016 special district measure, the library there remained open, managed by their library friends group, after April 1st, 2017, but only in the limited role of a reading library for several months.

Epilogue

In 2022 I was still volunteering at my local library. Telling my friend about it one day, he made a remark that led me to write a poem in his honor. A few months later, the poem led me to write a short essay. I continued to do my Monday volunteer shifts until August 2024.

OPENING THE LIBRARY ON MONDAY MORNINGS

(For James Ross Kelly)

"It sounds like there's a poem in there somewhere," he said,

Which is the sort of thing that poets say

Little realizing, perhaps, how they often disturb the world.

It is true that it pleases me that the key to the back door

Also opens the front door and how the books sit, shelved

In the dark, waiting for me to bring some light.

But now, well, every damned thing seems to have

A poem in it somewhere waiting for the right words

And my comfortable way of seeing things has gone from me.

On Monday mornings at 9:30 I unlock the back door at Myrtle Creek Library and step into a dimly lit back room. There are a few lights scattered about the building for nighttime security, but most have been turned off in order to save the city money on the power bill. Seeing the main room shelves with their books waiting in darkness is always a moment of anticipation, almost sacred, as if I should be genuflecting when I step inside the door. Every word in each of those books came into this place because a writer had the courage to fill a blank page with words. Here, in this small-town temple of knowledge and compassion, those carefully chosen words wait for me to turn on the lights.

In my weekly volunteer routine, I click the switches one-by-one: one for the office, two for the big room, one for the back storage closet, two more for the reading room and one each for the men's and women's restrooms. There is comfort and satisfaction in making my rounds, a matter of bringing both literal and metaphorical enlightenment to my little rural world which sits like a small green island in a sea of mountain ridges, not cut off from the world at large but, to some extent, sheltered from it.

There are thirty busy minutes between my arrival at the back door and ten o'clock, when the first patrons may arrive. The necessary tasks are simple and not terribly time-consuming, and although two of them can be done after opening, there are several of them.

The backdoor key also opens the front door, and that door has a small "Closed/Open" sign that I reverse. Although the library isn't officially open for another half hour, yet I don't mind letting someone in. This doesn't happen often but, when it does, it is usually someone in an urgent hurry to get to the restroom or a transient simply looking for warmth after a night out in the cold.

Just inside the front door is a small yard sign announcing our used book sale. The sale is a permanent fixture that used to be an annual event back when this library was part of a countywide public library system and was open forty hours per week, spread out over six days. Now this place is available twenty hours per week on four days and is staffed by volunteers like me and depends on grants, the used books and empty bottles and cans that our patrons drop off for us so that we can collect the ten-cent deposit. The sign gets planted out on the front lawn next to the much larger steel sign which reads:

> Friends of Myrtle Creek Library
> 100% Volunteer
> Blood, Sweat and Tears

I don't recall any blood being spilled in the process of reclaiming the town library, but there were, in fact, real tears shed when it finally closed, and it did take some hard work to get it reopened.

My favorite part of the mornings is sweeping the front walkway. For six months back in the 1970s I worked as a cleanup man for a local veneer plant, a surprisingly dangerous job. I'd been hired to replace the previous floor sweeper who had been killed while working beneath the machinery when someone unfortunately pushed a switch and left him a mangled corpse. It was satisfying work (as all of the most menial jobs always seem to be) and I enjoyed the freedom to move from place to place within the huge building while nearly everyone else stood in the same spot for ten hours endlessly repeating the same motions in obedience to the demands of the machinery. I was a young buck back then and now, in my dotage, I serenely wield my broom, secure in the knowledge that the only profit involved is cleanliness and that no one will notice the fruits of my brief labors. Like leadership, the results of essential work well done should go unremarked by those who benefit from it.

We have two small plastic hand baskets of the sort that are usually found stacked just inside the front door of a grocery market. These sometimes come in handy for returning books and CDs to the shelves but most often they are used for bringing books and newspapers in from the outdoor drop box. Our county's daily supplies us with a generous drop of five copies for each new edition. These go in the reading room and are really too many, considering that so few come by to read them but, after a few days, they do serve as free fire starters for some of our elderly patrons.

The newspaper did a feature article recently marking the fifth anniversary of the demise of our Douglas County Library System and the efforts to reopen all eleven of those libraries. It was good for the libraries to have a write-up and flattering to read the heroic portrayal of the work being done by the many library volunteers at work throughout the county. But there was little consideration of the tragic budget cuts and even more tragically failed property tax measure that killed the system. The piece also didn't mention that those libraries are now open to the public for about half of the hours that they had with county funding. The simple fact is that there has not been any adequate library service in the county for the past five years.

The busy Monday morning routine continues with a brief inspection of the restrooms (toilet seat up for the men's and down for the women's), checking the book drop-box books in, searching the shelves for reserved books, setting up the daily visitor record sheet and setting up the till.

I try to set up the cash register before anyone comes in, counting out the Federal Reserve notes and quarters carefully to make sure that the starting amount is always the same each day. There's a worrisome sense of responsibility that comes with handling the cash, not from an actual fear of theft or robbery but there is a weighty formality to the process of handling the economic lifeblood of this beloved place. But then, simply being there at work in the library is, after all, a responsible act.

The first patrons of the day are almost always some of our elderly neighbors. The mommies and toddlers come later, and the school-age kids show up after three. As with large swaths of rural America, we have a high percentage of elderly citizens along with a high percentage of poverty. As a result, many of the older folks who come in are poor people. But the most trying part of their lives seems to be loneliness and that, I think, is what most often brings them in to this warm and well-lit place where they can talk to friendly neighbors who just want to be helpful. More than half of those volunteers themselves are retirees who have arrived in our area relatively recently. It is, for them too, a way to counter isolation, to make friends among their fellow volunteers and among the library's patrons.

It seems odd to me now that it wasn't until I began working here that I realized that these common institutions are critically important to their communities not just as centers for study and entertainment but, more importantly, as antidotes to the twin plagues of isolation and alienation.

The Daily Yonder 2/17/23

Addendum: Campaign Lessons

Leadership Support

Local government support is essential for a library district tax-base measure to succeed. County commissions in Hood River County, Oregon and Klamath County, Oregon both supported their measures and both election efforts passed. When Klamath County's commissioners hired a new library director to replace a retiring director, they told the people who applied for the position that they expected whoever they hired to work with the group proposing the measure and to do so on their own time, since using "on-the-clock" county time would violate state law.

In both of the two Douglas County efforts all three commissioners were asked to support the measure and refused to do so. They were then asked to not oppose the measure and all three promised to not do so. In the 2016 effort one of the commissioners actively opposed the measure by touring city councils to assure them that the libraries would not actually close if the measure failed to pass.

All three commissioners in office during both the 2011 and 2016 efforts had received the bulk of their election campaign contributions from timber industry operators. That the commissioner who was serving as the library system's liaison during the 2011 effort was also the president of the O&C Counties Association, a group that was lobbying congress and suing the federal government to seek increased timber cutting levels seems a bit "fishy." He refused to support the measure in 2011 and subsequently said that he felt that passage of the measure would have hindered his efforts to lobby for continued federal subsidies.

Supporters

The Save Our Libraries PAC succeeded in obtaining the support of the county's daily newspaper, *The News-Review*. Also in support were the League of Women Voters Umpqua Valley and the Democratic Party of Douglas County. PAC members spoke to several local chambers of commerce and to nonpartisan social groups such as the Lion's Clubs, The Optimists and Rotarians. These club groups were not expected to take a stand for or against the measure but were open to learning about the measure. There were, in addition, businesses that helped. Dutch Brothers Coffee, Creative Images, Triple Oak Winery and Swanson Lumber all helped in their own ways.

In 2016, The Ford Family Foundation, a local 501(c)3 nonprofit, through a grant to the Douglas County Library Foundation, funded a generalized "Libraries Matter" campaign which did not directly support the campaign, but which paid for banners, newspaper advertising and the creation of a video touting the importance of libraries for their communities.

Opposition

Efforts to speak to the Republican Party of Douglas County about the measure were refused and the RPDC central committee later voted to finance signage in opposition to the measure. This signage did not use the word "library" but named the measure by its ballot number, which, according to the chairman of the RPDC central committee was a deliberate choice. Speaking to the Lumber and Sawmill Workers, Local 2949 did not result in an endorsement.

About a month out from the election, a local weekly conservative newspaper, *The Beacon,* Roseburg, came out against the measure and accused the PAC of lying to the public by claiming that the libraries would close if the measure didn't pass.

Around that time, a "Forum" about the measure was announced by an informal group of anti-taxation opponents. The SOL PAC was not invited to speak at the event and when a few of the PAC's members attended, they were later accused in an email chain letter of intimidating the speakers by asking why no proponents of the measure had been invited to speak.

Unsubstantiated claims from opponents, when made close to an impending election, are always difficult to refute in time to help correct the record. This is a common political strategy and one to be expected.

Tactics

Raising awareness of the problems that the system was facing was difficult, in part because it seemed unimaginable to so many and in part because of the drop-off in library use that occurred as the hours were incrementally shaved over the years in response to the annual budget cuts. "It's never open," was one recurring complaint.

A few "no" voters later said that, being used to voting down tax measures for school districts which failed but were later passed at a lower rate, they voted against, expecting that same thing to happen for the county library system.

Artist Robert Bell, of Dillard Oregon, designed a simple sign in red, white and blue reading "Library Yes" with the traditional check mark symbol. These were printed in both lawn sign size and in a larger format and were distributed around the county by PAC members.

Bell also designed a bumper sticker reading, "I Support My Library" and listing the Douglas County Library Foundation's URL. Over one thousand of these were printed and distributed in DCLS libraries and at public events and became a fairly common sight locally. He also hand-painted an eight-foot canvas banner using the same design, which was used for information tabling. Bell also designed a placard reading "Save 'em or Kiss 'em goodbye Library Yes," which featured the red lipstick impression of a kiss.

Both the DCLF and the Save Our Libraries PAC created and distributed flyers and other materials including a small tabletop cardboard A-frame folded sign for restaurant use.

Information tables were set up at public events, including the annual Spring Fair and the Douglas County Fair. The Canyonville Farmers Market donated booth space for weekly informational tabling. PAC members wrote guest columns and letters to the editor for the local daily newspaper and weeklies.

On October 31st, 2016, the PAC participated in Roseburg's annual Neewollah Parade leading a small contingent of costumed trick-or-treating children behind the "I Support My Library" canvas banner. The children carried little child-sized picket signs reading: Free Books for All Kids, We Love Storytime, Libraries Are Nice Places, We ♥ Libraries, and Librarians Like Kids.

Polling

Polls conducted for both efforts were consistent with each other and accurate when it came to the outcome of the election. With about 45% of the respondents willing to vote in favor and between 10% to 20% undecided it seemed that, should half of the undecided voters break in favor, there was a real chance of passage for the measure. The final outcome was 45% of the votes being in favor with 55% opposing it. The vote in three of the county's cities—Roseburg, Drain and Reedsport—were in favor of the measure and all three cities later voted to establish their own independent tax-supported library districts.

One of the three county commissioners later said that we'd done much better than he or his two fellow commissioners had expected. Given that the 2016 general election vote for Donald J. Trump that same day ran 64.6% in his favor in Douglas County, it seems that libraries are generally well regarded in the county and that a generalized anti-taxation sentiment was what drove the "no" vote.

By the same author:
OVERSTORY ZERO:
REAL LIFE IN TIMBER COUNTRY
2nd Edition

Robert Leo Heilman's award-winning essay collection about work, family, community, and the land is back in print, revised and expanded with ten new pieces added about small-town life in timber country.

Sylph Maid Books

P.O. Box 932
Myrtle Creek, OR 97457 U.S.A.
Phone: (541) 863-5069

By the same author:
THE WORLD POOL
A LITERARY VARIETY

    The World Pool is an eclectic collection of short works selected from the author's thirty years' worth of freelance writing, 1985–2015. This literary variety show brings readers a swirl of essays, articles, vignettes and short stories that range across the personal, historical and fanciful worlds of life. Here's your chance to jump aboard this merry-go-round of thoughts and stories for a brief tour through so much of what it means to be human.

Sylph Maid Books

P.O. Box 932
Myrtle Creek, OR 97457 U.S.A.
Phone: (541) 863-5069

By the same author:
CHILDREN OF DEATH

In this book-length meditation, the author takes us along on his journeys retracing the migrations of his family from Alsace, France to Russia in 1810 and on to Kazakhstan and the American Midwest. Along the way, he brings us a history of the times and the fates of a farming family in search of land, freedom and security through the troubled times of the Reign of Terror, the Russian Revolution, famines, Stalin's purges and World War II.

Sylph Maid Books

P.O. Box 932
Myrtle Creek, OR 97457 U.S.A.
Phone: (541) 863-5069